AF582784

Dedication

This book is dedicated to you at the very first, because you are the main reason I am writing this book. The education is something begin from us first than around us. It's like connecting the dots.

Other than you by son, who inspired me in a very unique way to write this book, may be through him and this book I could be a reason to make a change, and as we say an act of goodness creates an endless ripples.

Lastly my loved ones and everyone around me who has given so much to me as support to write this book, as content, as an inspiration that there are plenty of things in our hand which can make this world a better place to live.

May the endless positive changes begin from us and especially from your life.

Table of Contents

Introduction

"Educating the mind without educating the heart is no education at all."

Aristotle

I often ask a question to myself that, if the education is for our betterment, so, are we actually becoming better. Off course our primary focus is to become a better version of ourselves, just like the iphone 16 should be better than I phone 15 may be? So many such questions.

So, Firstly, how this book is going to be helpful for you and for your loved once too? Whatever has helped me a lot, in my journey of life, I will be trying to do my best here, and I really believe I will be able to solve every question regarding to life and education for sure.

We all have a perception of education as what it is actually, As per Google too, basically, education means the teaching, and training of people especially in schools.

Transformation of knowledge and information overall from one to another is also considered as education. A big controversy is present in the whole world on this topic of what the actual definition of education is. Let's talk about it through a story.

In a classroom there were two 6 years young and cute students Yogesh and Rajesh, their teacher was trying to teach addition to students, the teacher called Yogesh and Rajesh both in front, gave 5 pencils to Rajesh and asked Rajesh to give 2 pencils to Yogesh, he gave, then asked again to give the remaining 3 pencils to Yogesh, he gave 3 pencils, and asked Yogesh

"Son Rajesh gave you 2 pencils once and then 3 pencils again, how many pencils do you have now?"

Yogesh replied

"6 mam"

He had a curious look on his face, and the teacher did too, she thought the kids misunderstood, so she repeated the process and asked

"My son, listen to me carefully, Your friend Rajesh gave you 2 pencils first, and in the second time he gave you 3 more pencils, how many pencils do you have now?",

"6 again mam"

Yogesh replied.

Mam got confused now, and thought, there has to be something I might be missing, how and why kids are confused, it's a wonderful sign of a good teacher, she interchanged the objects from pencils to pens. She again told Rajesh to repeat the process and give 2 pens first to Yogesh and then 3 pens the second time, Rajesh did that. The teacher asked the same question again to Yogesh

"My son, Listen to me carefully more this time okay? Rajesh gave you 2 pens first and then 3 pens in the second time. How many pens do you have now?"

After a moment Yogesh said

"5 pens Mam".

Now even with the right answer mam got confused again, if he can count it this easily then what was the issue previously? So out of curiosity, she asked Rajesh to repeat the process with pencils again. Rajesh being a very good student, Rajesh gave 2 pencils to Yogesh and then 3 pencils to Yogesh in second time, now teacher asked again

"Yogesh listen to me very carefully this time son, Rajesh gave you 2 pencils first and 3 pencils in the second time, how many pencils you have now?",

Yogesh said

"6 mam",

Now mam was thinking Yogesh is an intelligent kid, why is he behaving as if he is not understanding it properly, instead of trying to explain that how the addition happens, now she asked Yogesh

"if Rajesh is giving you 2 and 3 pens you are saying 5, but if he is giving you 2 and 3 pencils you are saying 6, why?"

An exact approach.

Yogesh with an innocent smile said,

“Mam, because I have got one more pencil in my pocket, and you were asking how many pencils I have, so 2 pencils, 3 pencils, and 1 more pencil from my pocket, I have 6 in total. Am I doing addition wrong mam?”

So cute! But Above this cuteness, so many things can be learned from this one.

1. The meaning of education is diverse. Completely depends upon perspective.
2. If one is right, it doesn’t mean the other one is wrong.
3. We should be able to see from other’s perspectives too.
4. The teacher plays a vital role in children’s lives.
5. And the most important of all, the person we have in front, is having something with him, or in him, that is something we are not aware of, that is something which is either hidden or either we do not have intentions of knowing about, as we stay so busy in telling them our perspective, once we get to know what they have inside of them, or with them, once we understand that, then and only then we can understand the person in front is right too.

But before getting to our first topic here, with more focus, which is education, Let me say a pleasant hello to everyone who is reading this book, and got themselves this far, well Congratulations you are among the 0.1% of the people who are willing to do something good, willing to learn, and willing to read too, all of it simultaneously, I am Rahul Bajad and have written this book with a collection of facts figures, actual life problems through life experiences, and a solution-oriented perspective, all wrapped up through stories too, We will be covering almost everything from my perspective one by one. Reading this book will surely be able to benefit you to get apart from the rat race and of course, and will give you a more pleasant and successful life. I wish you a happy reading and a powerful wisdom.

Big Thanks!

Rahul Bajad

Education

Let's get to our first topic Education, from my perspective too, it has a diversified meaning, and what I have learned so far is, the meaning of education completely depends upon the purpose of education, no matter the age group of somebody who is educating. The syllabus, the curriculum, and the design of the education system. It all depends on the purpose of education and this is where I want you to put your focus. And why it is necessary.

To understand it we may need to get an understanding of the evolution of purposes with the evolution of education. Where the root of everything is lying. Out of 87 lakhs of species, no matter how intelligent they are, how much IQ level they have. This education is something almost all of them want, this is where it all began.

Let's take the example of a giraffe, the moment a calf is born, the giraffe gives birth to the calf in a standing position, and the calf falls from 5 feet the moment it leaves the mother's body. And within an hour of birth, the calf is in the position of standing and walking too. But this is somehow only the giraffes know. And the first lesson of education of life began. The giraffe plays the role of a teacher here, and the calf is playing student. The giraffes even kick their kid calves so that they should not just sit on the ground, and make a movement there this is how the first lesson is taught, and the calf takes his first step to life.

If I ask you what is the purpose of this education? The answer is crystal clear, the giraffes want their kid to walk, not just that they want their kid to be the best version of him. They don't have language in between them, neither the giraffes can speak, nor the calf can listen. But the lesson is there, the education is there, the purpose is there.

Now I want you to compare the same situation with the education system, the purposes. Education has a wide range here. Education in pre-primary, primary, secondary, senior, college, and so on. Different levels of education, and different levels of purposes too. There are two purposes. One is the main purpose of education from pre-primary to post-graduate even after post-graduation, there is an education system, pattern, and above it "purpose". The second purpose is hidden often.

This purpose is something that has made the highest intelligent breads of the world not more than puppets mostly. Maybe some people may not agree with me completely but to prove this statement of mine, and to give you an idea of how am I able to compare humans to puppets can be done through another question though. Let me ask you this, intelligence means the capability of understanding, and learning, so that we can make better decisions, right? And there is no question that we are blessed, and we have developed a better intelligence than so many creatures and species around the world right? Our senses are developed far better than any other species.

Let's take the example of a dog, can we make better decisions than a dog? Some would say what kind of question is this, take it like this, suppose we give something to a dog to eat, the dog will be able to decide whether to eat it or not with just one single sniff, within a moment he will either take the food, or he will reject it. Now do the same thing for the humans, put 100's of food in front of them, will they be able to decide it in a moment? Or with a sniff? Even for hours of discussion my friend they won't be able to tell with 100% surety that this thing should be eaten or not. Or at least again a kind of controversy may appear whether the thing in front is eatable or not. So the question arises is, if we have developed intelligence and senses, does a dog have better senses than us? Or a better understanding than us? The answer is NO! But in a more prior sense, I want your focus to be on it. Is there something that is diverting us to not being able to decide as clearly as a dog about FOOD? And again the answer is yes, there is, and if we are not able to decide too, as quick and as clear as that single sniff as a dog. Then there is something of ours, which is getting controlled by someone else, I believe this is a definition of a puppet. Am I wrong here?

Trust me, the very same thing is true for education too, the purpose is overall playing the most important and dangerous role of diluting the true meaning of education here.

Practical solution based approach

Although we will be doing this with each chapter, but before that, let's talk about a practical and solution-based approach here, to take good decisions, we need a good wisdom in priority, and to develop that, what do we need? At least plenty of to think, or making our kids busy in early age, is it a good idea?

So one example of solution oriented approach could be, Like in India, the average age of students admitted to school mostly in private schools I should be saying here is 2 and half years as a beginning for a pre-primary section of the school.

How much a kid can understand or study at this age? There are schools around the globe which has a minimum age of 7 years before getting to school admission. This means before getting to the age of 7 years, the kid is not allowed in school, they believe the kid should live his life, and stay happy at home, with no study pressure, no schooling pressure should be there before he is 7. According to the Oregon home education network, you must register your child with the state if they will be at least 7 years old by 1st September. If we go with facts and figures, this has been considered as part of the most powerful education system.

Before getting to any powerful conclusion, let's take this book as a step-by step guide, to clear our focus through education. I want you to do a simple task here, List down every education course or syllabus you have been through. Or your loved ones have been through. Example.

1. Pre-primary section
2. Primary school
3. Secondary school
4. ....And such.

Till graduation or other than graduation whatever you consider as an education course, then I want you to note down the purpose of each education course you have done, and please compare each educational course's purpose. If it has changed or not. Please try to be the best honest from you inside. Warning it is not going to be easy, especially for those who are just following somebody else's direction in education now.

I want you to ask yourself, why did you take that education? What was your purpose behind that course? List them out, and then continue with the book please.

Now, I should be honest with you when I thought of this book, I was selfish initially for my kid, but once I got to the truth, while I was studying to make this book too, so now I am writing this book for all of you, considering you all are my family.

Not that trustable statement?

When you ask somebody, whose nation is this, the reply is going to be simple.

"IT'S OURS!"

Ask the same people whose city is this? Same answer will appear.

"IT'S OURS!"

And without a wonder, ask the same people, whose family is this. He will be saying.

"IT's mine"

Or in a sense of humour, ask one of the husband here, whose wife is this? Do you wonder what he would say?

"She's mine"

And whenever we say it's mine we take the responsibility of them, just like the husband takes good care of his wife, as he feels responsible for her. And in a contrasting way, the situation of everything which is of OURS. Is far more different than everything which is MINE.

Take example of your home where you're family lives, and the city you live, which one is cleaner? Home or city? Off course home.

Humorously, which is better situation your wife? Or you're Street?

Humour is always easy to remember as it leaves more of emotional content on our mind.

So I would say again, I am writing this book for you as MY family not OUR family, and everyone around us as MY own family not OUR family. Through this deed, I am trying to fulfil my responsibility towards the whole world as MY family. Because of these all, if I could be able to do any good to society, I owe this to the world, with sincere intentions to make a better world for us, all as my family and you all as my loved ones.

I can promise you this, if you could get to the end of the book and could get the book content inside you, you will be able to do wonders in the world and not just that.

"An act of goodness creates an endless ripple."

- Rahul Bajad

Overall what I am trying to conclude here, through many of mine and many educated experienced people, we will be talking about the primary 9 necessary aspects of education which are a must in education, and a priority too. I believe these nine aspects should be a part of the education system if they cannot be included through the government of ours or any of the country. We can include that for ourselves and our loved ones around us. We are going to discuss them one by one here, as per the content, I welcome you all on this small powerful journey of a making whole new world of goodness. With a humbler request that, please be with me with a highlighter. And to create a better place to live, to create a better world. Let's go through our common SHARP WISH, through these 9 necessities as: -

SHARP WISH

S Survival

H Humanity,

A Attitude

R Responsibility

P Purpose

W Wisdom

I Identity

S Social Animal

H Honesty

They are Necessities, Always remember there could be a PLAN B, but I am sure there is NO PLANet B. So Let's make this world a better place to live, and

Let there be lights.

Necessity 2

Wisdom

"Never mistake knowledge for wisdom, one helps you to make a living, and the other helps you to make a life."

- Sandra Carey

I know what you might be thinking, but it's not a printing mistake, there is a reason that I had to take chapter as necessity 2 first. Throughout the journey, I will be leaving this to you, where do you want to take Chapter 1 as a priority, or Chapter 2? When you will complete the chapter 2, you will know where to place this. Let's begin.

People often consider knowledge is the powerful thing in education, but from my perspective. I really wish after reading this chapter from your perspective too wisdom is way above all.

Information, Knowledge and Wisdom are not same.

Before that, the wisdom. Let's first discuss it, it is a generation of information technology. Everything is available at your fingertips. Whatever you want to know, information about that thing or at least similar information to what you want is available on the Internet. But that is information. If we get to the definition of information is a little different if you Google the word information it will say knowledge or facts. What I am trying to say is it is not true. The language is a very limited thing to explain something sometimes. The information is overall and noun form of a verb called inform. If I am informing something of somebody or something, this means that I am saying something that has particular data from my perspective, just a set of words somebody saying can be considered as information. Just like a paper stick on a notice board, there could be something written on it. But similar to the people it is not necessary that the person who was informing him is going to read it.

In a contrasting way, knowledge is something different from this. Suppose information is here in front of me and I am taking it. If I am not taking it, then it is just an information, but if I am taking it myself, If I am learning through that information. Then we can make another statement that knowledge is here. This can be called as knowledge. So for the information to become knowledge it is a requirement that it has to get to the person, To Whom

It May Concern. And the person is trying to have intentions of learning through that. Although intentions of learning are really big terms to mention over here but I believe this much is enough to understand the difference between information and knowledge.

There is one more term which is above knowledge and we call it wisdom in English. In India, there is a similar term, not the exact one as the language is always limited. We call here buddhi (Wisdom). This wisdom is very different the knowledge and information though it can be gained through these too. Let's try to understand the concept through an example.

Suppose a teacher is trying to teach a student that 2 + 2 is 4. To teach this concept teacher takes four pencils to explain it utilizing 2 pencils plus two pencils is equal to 4 pencils. Whatever the teacher has said so far is a kind of information that has been given to students.

Now after this information delivery. If the students are listening to it and trying to have the intention to learn through that only those students are going to be knowledgeable through this information. Every student who is not mentally present in the class is not going to understand this concept. So knowledge will be built only into those were have intentions to learn. And as you and I both can say right now, teachers should try to spread knowledge not information. The difference here is those who got the concept of this information may be able to utilize this knowledge. Those who didn't take this concept as information are not going to utilize it and of course, they will not be able to.

Now take another situation over here, now to those students, who were able to successfully convert the information into knowledge. Suppose any of it is trying to do the same with his copies books pens bags school class table chairs and everything around him. Now they are utilizing their knowledge. The student who is trying to calculate everything has calculated 4 books as two books 2 + 2 books is equal to 4 books. In the later that day, he again calculated the books that were books plus two books and he stopped there, as there were no four books, there were only three books. So he found out one book was missing because the sum was not 4. And he tries to find it. Once he tried it he was somehow able to find it too. Now whatever knowledge he has taken he is trying to convert this knowledge with some good deed. Please highlight good deed here. This ability to convert knowledge is called wisdom. And this is not a onetime thing, it's a life long journey.

"Wisdom is not a product of schooling but of the

Lifelong attempt to acquire it."

- Albert Einstein

Once I met a teacher who used to teach up to secondary classes 8th class. She was setting up the question paper at home. She had to set question papers for all the classes. A few question papers were on the table, which were ready to send,

I asked her out of curiosity

"Can I have a look at them?"

She said

"Yes of course"

The question papers were there with the books where the questions had been taken. They were very simple and as it is written in the book. Mostly first and the second questions were her choice. I asked her

"Don't you think you should think out of the box the question paper you are setting is too easy these are the simple questions of every chapter?"

She was looking at me with a smile on her face and said

"You think this is easy, almost half of the class will not be able to solve this one as well, and if I'll be thinking out of the box, then I may have 90% of the students failed in the class, as a result so many questions from the parents school staff principal mam and as a result, I may lose my job then"

I was confused a little with this, and said

"If children will read any of the chapter once or twice, I believe they will be able to answer it easily, then why will they fail"

And she said

"There are so many things, I tried to explain them chapter by chapter, most of the time they are not interested in learning, we have to shout on them so that they could focus on study, but somehow they are not that so much interested in learning, they don't find this interesting, and after getting to home none of them almost are going to see read or revise chapter what they have learnt, and the kids are too young to understand, they almost forget everything till there exam time or test what they Read 2 months ago two weeks ago or something"

So I asked her

“Doesn't the school have revision classes?"

And what she replied is something you will find weird too

"Not just revision classes, before the exams on the name of tests, we give them all the questions which are going to be asked in the main exam"

I stopped there in the middle

"Don't you think this is bad, it is a kind of cheating, playing with the future of a student's?"

And what she said

"Try to understand, if I will not be able to get most of the students passed then I have to lose my job, I have to get the students passed"

Whether the students understand or don't understand does not matter, what matters is that the student should pass so that the job of the teacher is safe, not just from the discussion, I have talked with most of the teachers got a similar feeling that the purpose is to earn living, and to do that the teacher have to be successful in their work, and by successful they are making a sense out of nothing, they believe that should be a mark pass in the mark sheet anyhow is their success.

Don't you think knowledge or wisdom should be the primary focus of a teacher? If Students are not able to gain knowledge through their information, then the whole information method and the teaching makes no sense. And if there is no knowledge, converting knowledge into wisdom is going to be a myth.

Wisdom is above knowledge and information, from my perspective, it is something that is the requirement. If we look around us self the whole education system focuses on information as a priority.

Most of the students either understand or not it doesn't matter for them. If you talk to almost any of the teachers in any of the schools they are going to say we have to complete the syllabus these chapters are finished these chapters are something I have to complete. Such lines are being used by most of the teachers around us. I have not heard one single line from any of the teachers saying if students are not understanding then it is useless for me to teach. Most of them are going to say I did my part now, if students are not studying that is their fault.

How in world, this is going to take kids towards wisdom? Let's go through this with another real life example.

My son once was mugging up some sentences for his homework loudly

"THE LARGEST MOON OF SATURN IS NAMED TITAN, THE LARGEST MOO..."

My father stopped him in the middle and said

"My son, you are supposed to learn this not to mug this up"

The kid with a weird expression on his face asked,

"Learn, what do you mean by it daadu."

His grandfather explained

“Just try to understand the meaning of it, and say the same thing in your words, not just mug it up”,

An 8 year could still hardly understand it, so he again asked what you mean, so grandfather laughed a little and gave his second best shot explaining it with a simple question

“Did you understand what you were mugging?”

“Noo,”

He said,

Than Daadu explained the meaning of it in his own words of course in Hindi, so after some time, Even after a little understanding between ‘learning’ and ‘mugging’, he was again mugging up the sentence and with similar volume

“THE LARGEST MOON OF SATURN IS NA....”

I stopped him in the middle

“WAIT, WAIT, WAIT, Didn’t your Daadu just explained you not to mug these up,”

I said,

He replied

“Daadu could be right papa, but I am not going to get marks if I will not write it, in the same manner, it is written here”

I had goose bumps. Is what marks are something education is made for?

Seriously? This is the story of every kid, ask them, and is this what we are wanting our kids to get from school?

Something isn't right here, If something isn't right, than there has to be something which is wrong, let's try to find out through this story.

A few kids from school got a chance to go on a camping trip, they went there and decided to camp around a river area, they spent their day playing with the environment, they found so many animals there too, made a campfire there and spent their night there, after a while they got back to school, things seem pretty simple, right?

Let's see another perspective here, there were a few animals specially a family of foxes who used to live near a river, that was a regular day there she was cleaning her kids few were playing around, and a few were drinking water, suddenly a bus stopped there and few other creatures got down from the bus, who were bigger than them, and was shouting and making noises, the fox and her kids instantly got a little away from there behind a tree in distance. They all were scared as the kids who got down from the bus were teasing the butterflies, they were bothering fishes, fishes also were making distance from them, and every animal was thinking about how much time they would bother us. But no animal tried to get to them, as they all were scared of kids, they even waited at night for their place to clean up so that they all could sleep, but when they roamed around, they saw fire sticks into the hands of those humans, they got scared more, and everybody around left that place but humans. It is a possibility, right?

Let's take it in a deeper possible way, the fox went to the other animals too, and asked the same question, that we animals are way more powerful than these humans, is the fox right here? She asked the lion too, "The elephant is a giant animal way more powerful than humans, and can take so many humans down. The leopard is so fast that no human will ever be able to run even around its acceleration. Even the lion is powerful enough to take down any other humans, they don't have claws like us, they don't have teeth like us, nobody is as powerful as us, and nobody is as fast as us. Then how dare they are to scare us?"

Fox is right here, what is separating us from animals? It's our intelligence, right? Our intelligence is separating us from animals, allowed to think far further than an animal can ever do. My point here is if a kid or us, if any of us as humans are doing something that doesn't involve our intelligence what's the use of it, aren't we animals too? Doing the same thing again and again, learning nothing new, feeling boar and disgusting with the mechanical life we have.

Waiting for the weekend to come and refresh ourselves again so that we can do the same thing we have been doing for years? If this is education or this is where our life is leading, don't you think we should be doing something about it too?

It's simple, we are different from animals as we have got powerful intelligence, and brains, we can use our wisdom, but wisdom has just become a word, the weird truth is, it wasn't like that from the beginning, when this whole education system was created, I am talking about the time of something 1500BCE when guru Vashishtha and guru Vishwa Mitra. Who designed this education system including all the aspects we have now too, The Gurukuls focused on holistic education including subjects like vedas, mathematics, astronomy, philosophy, ethics, politics, and warfare. Each gurukul had its own specific curriculum, tailored to the needs and interests of the students and the expertise of the guru (teacher). While there were common foundational subjects, the sullabus could vary from one Gurukul to another based on the guru's specialization and the needs of the students

But then something changed in the middle of it, you might know why did it change? The system got changed in the name of development and growth, There is something that we all should know, that there are some people on earth who don't want us to use our intelligence that's the reason our syllabus and the whole schooling system have been modified. And this system has got so many loopholes around it.

"The only true wisdom is in knowing you know nothing."

\- Socrates

The word experiment came from a desire for improvement. And this word improvement has got a lot in itself. What I mean is these are two lines that have a world of difference in their meaning respectively, one work is done, and the second is work is being done. The first one is saying about the completion of something, and the second one is saying about the process. And in our nature the almighty has made plenty of processes, as an example the evolution of the earth is a process, right? It is not done it is still evolving, and this is a forever process, it can't be ever said that evolution is done now, this is the limit now the earth is perfect how it should be, is it possible?

The same is true with us as well, we are evolving whatever we are now is not the final destination the human is a name of process, a process of evolution. So one thing is surely true we are not the best version of ourselves, there is more to happen with us. But if one person among us comes and says

"Okay people, I have studied it enough, here are the notes, I know everything and I have written every process in steps that we should all follow".

And people start following those notes, I am not comparing laws or theories, but a thought process. The whole world has made parts of themselves and calls themselves countries, they all have got some coloured clothes with them, they call it flag and suddenly emotions get stuck to it. Everybody has made a particular syllabus of themselves, which they are making every teacher and every student to follow. But the fact is still the same seeing the present, deciding which process is right, or which process is wrong is a big question in itself, because at last IT IS A PROCESS, it has to evolve. We have to keep on experimenting with it.

But have we ever thought if we will stop experimenting and consider that whatever system has been made is good enough now? What may happen after that? You can see the situation of the education system now.

Once I got a chance to meet an experienced language trainer Mr. Binod sir was working with a famous institute. He was teaching a class with something different, even I didn't even see a syllabus anywhere. Few students were taking an interest few were not, but he was digging up and up with the same focus, and something remarkable. When the class got over I couldn't stop myself and asked him

"Binod sir, don't you think the thing we were discussing in the class was something very unique, what inspired you for this teaching methodology."

And his reply is still in my ears

"Look Rahul, I believe the word GURU doesn't mean teacher, it means the power who takes one from GU which means darkness or dark, to RU which means lightness or light, and for a person to get to light he has to explore, and the only way to find that is to think out of the box, I want them to think out of the box, and if I will remain in the box, not thinking anything new, then how will they think out of box?"

Trust me he is so right, the method of unboxing the idea may come good sometimes, but sometimes it may not, from my perspective the way the education system is working is not coming out well. So from my perspective thinking out of the box is important, to find a better way. This is how the experiments happen right? A few things I came to know that day too, everybody of us is trying to find a way or path. So for me too, I know a path that I explored by myself, but

1. That was my dark path, and so the path is mine too, and because of that path will not help any other student,
2. With time every path changes, nothing is permanent, and nor the path is, And
3. Most importantly every being in the world may seem similar but unique in their own, and because of this uniqueness, the method has to be unique.

I mean come on, consider an example of hospitals or doctors, if a case for admission comes to a doctor, first they ask to fill in the admission details on a form, then they ask questions, try to understand the person, the issues what he is facing, the study it, they try to diagnose through it, they even perform physical and mental tests than they decide the treatment and even, after that treatment they maintain and record every progress with the person and call him a subject. If the treatment doesn't work properly they study it further, change the treatment, and do their best to solve the case, and still, they call it PRACTICE.

And if we even dare to compare the same with education, schools, or institutes? There is an inquiry appearing for admission, first, the counter desk will convince you why the institute or the school is best suitable for you. They say they are willing to know the kid, they have got forms to be filled, they have tests too, almost all of them pretend as if they are diagnosing, and hence treatment is prepared, the methods as how to treat the kid is prepared, and do you know the kind of treatment they prepared for every unique student? that nobody is unique every kid is the same, every treatment is the same, one teacher one subject, one blackboard, and the teacher treats every student with the same treatment, can we treat every disease through only one treatment say paracetamol? Now the record of every treatment is here too, the reports are here too, and all the kids who have faced the same treatment aren't allowed to question the diagnosis. Do you know the reason why, because the reports are almost fake, in India under right to education up to the age of 14 years is guaranteed as a fundamental right under Article 21A of the Constitution of India and a student cannot be failed up to 8th Class?

Let's get to the conclusion now, definitely the system is too big to change, but aren't we too small to make changes for our own kids, at the minimum? Let's try to the same for our kids, every child is unique, every child is born with different unique capabilities and different possibilities, let's not measure them with the same measurement scale, let's give them enough of space to explore their own path to wisdom, definitely we will always be there for them. At least we can observe different treatments for our child.

1. In so many countries such as Finland the minimum age to get admission in school is 7 years, they do wonders in international testing competitions.
2. There are places where there is no conduction of exams till the age of 13.
3. There are places where there is no school bags.
4. There are places where, humbleness is a top most priority in school
5. There are places where there is punishment to clean their own class if you get late to school, every students group cleans their own classes still. Teaching survival in priority.
6. There are places where discipline is priority.
7. There are places where privatization of school isn't allowed.
8. There are places where coaching classes aren't allowed.

9. There are places where education isn't business.

And I am pretty sure, my family's education isn't business, you are part of my family, let's try a little bit more to make the place better for our kids to learn more. A kid have got unbelievable capabilities in them, and to discover that they would need proper wisdom, You can always count how many seeds a fruit may have, but you will never be able to count how many seeds one seed can produce.

"I would rather prefer a seed to send in soil, instead on a marble finish floor, a seed needs environment to grow its best, and it's our responsibility to do so, whether they are our kids or seeds."

- Rahul Bajad

So let's make surroundings of our kids or us to be the best place to grow their wisdom, just like a tree grows to its max if the seeds gets the proper environment and proper care, there is no doubt with that. Same is true for our kid, I know you care a lot about your kid, and it's time to rethink about the environment, at least the education we are depending upon.

I wish you and your loved ones the most powerful wisdom ever possible.

Necessity 1

Identity

"To be yourself in a world that is constantly trying to make you something else is the greatest accomplishment."

- Ralph Waldo Emerson.

There are big questions in the world, who are we? Instead of us, you can put me too. Who am I? And the bigger question is, why it is necessary to know the answer to this question?

We all have a common desire in ourselves, the desire to keep our self-safe. This desire to keep our self-safe is something which we have learned from our experiences and our elders, and above it, our ancestors too when we were evolving from monkeys to humans, actually not just us, almost every creature in the world, has this tendency in themselves, coded now, of keeping themselves safe. And to save themselves they do everything from all of their capabilities. Whatever they have got in them, they put everything to keep themselves. What they try to save, considering not just them, it is their identity. A dog tries to save himself, a cat does the same, every animal every insect and we do it too.

When we were kids, if we felt threat by anything, we starts to try to save ourselves, even from a slap or something, to save ourselves. This goes on and on, even till the end of our life, it is with us. We want ourselves to be saved, and our whole capability is utilized to save so. That becomes us. Usually our identity.

Not just that, our capabilities become our power later on, we start utilizing our capabilities, and powers to fulfil our desires, and our wishes, and this also becomes our identity. Now whosoever has got whatsoever in his hands as power, as capabilities he starts utilizing it considering his own identity right, and considers his deeds as the best possible solution of everything? Try to look at all the good, great, and bad deeds all around the world ever have happened. A soldier kills somebody for a reason, while killing he is utilizing all of his strength, skills, powers, knowledge, and wisdom to complete this killing. This killing is justified under his identity, as he is a soldier. Whatever he does becomes a powerful thing for the nation. The family feels proud of him. The whole world is proud of him. Indeed it is a thing to be proud of if whatever life he has taken is or in whatever circumstances he made his best possible wise decision.

The same thing is true for a criminal, a killer, he uses all of his capabilities, his whole power to commit a crime, to take somebody's life, whatever he has learned so far from his own experiences, his skills, his knowledge and wisdom all of it has been utilized to commit the crime, or we can say, to do his deed. Whoever he is, he uses everything for his identity, he lies for his identity, and he does everything and anything possible for his identity. Whether that identity is right, wrong, good, bad, or worse. I am trying to say is, everything is justified under this identity. This identity has taken humanity to the next level. We all have become way different than every other creature in this world. As I often say, out of 87lacs of creatures we humans have developed this identity in such a manner that the worst possible side effect has popped up.

From the birth of the kid, his religion is decided, his country is decided, his state, his city, his food priorities, language, each and everything is decided by parents, whether right or wrong, big or small. He makes his identity through everything he gets from his environment and internal desires he builds his identity according to them.

"Nothing of me is Original, I am the combined effort of everyone I have ever known"

- Chuck Palahniuk

From all the stories I have heard so far even about all the gods, all the legends, and all. The story of a caveman, how he takes care of his food, and how he saves himself from other creatures. He uses all of his capabilities, and becomes successful at what he is.

Then further more few centuries later, couple more warriors popped up, who used all of their capabilities and developed skills through that, used it for their necessities, their security, and now for their entertainment too. Now hunting was not just for food it has become fun too, taking life of something or somebody became their identity and they have developed this identity of superiority over other creatures considering their intelligence.

Now this intelligence got against them, their whole system of considering themselves superior to other creatures has taken a different form of identity dilemma. Now humans have categorized themselves into different identities, and they started killing each other's in the name of identities. To put one's identity on the other, to get this feeling of superiority of one identity to another identity. They developed other things, as archery, swords, guns, then cannons, and they made strategies to take one identity to another.

The basic were still the same, the caveman had a kind of intelligence that intelligence was a skill set which all has been utilized to save his identity. The situation is still the same, but the level of intelligence has taken a whole new different situation here. It has taken advanced forms here. So this habit of humans of taking their identity at the top of everything has taken itself to a different level. Far away from weapons.

Initially, the fight was with their hands, then their skill set through weapons, but now, the fight has utilized the meaning of intelligence. This intelligence is very dangerous. Because the weapon is changing with intelligence, guns, AK47s, machine guns, tanks, missiles, air carriers, sea, land, and air, everywhere. The humans are using every bit of their intelligence to take down another identity, and to take their own identities to a superior level.

This presents how our capabilities can be used in a positive way. Now let's try to understand a different perspective on how our capabilities are being used in a little negative way too. Take an example of a kid.

Once I was in my parent's teacher meeting day. My kid complained that he was in a fight the day before yesterday with one of his classmates. Although I don't believe in many things, as they are kids, whenever a kid complains about anything, they are looking for support often. This support decides the future path of the child. If we are supporting a good deed, it's like a good seed, similarly good will be happening, it will grow in good and it will give well as a tree of all seasons. But if the seed is bad, somehow, we may have supported a bad deed, then a bad may happen, and it also grows similarly, off course the definition of good bad right wrong is having a vast meaning in itself, let's get into it later.

So I decided to talk to mam about what may have happened, I went there, my kid was not in favour of the talk, to mam about it. Of course, it sounds as if I may be supporting my kid. When I got to her, and asked her, she didn't remember the name of my kid, and she didn't know about what happened there that day initially, but she replied with a kind of statement

"Sir something happened that day for sure, your kid was crying a lot, and these two kids were fighting. He even got beaten by the other kid his head, students were saying that the other student threw your kid towards the table, and he got hit through him and table, we took him to the medical department here, and he stopped crying after sometime. Took other classes later the same day."

As he was able to study so off course that was not that hard hit, but he was still in pain a little, I came to know when he sleeps. He touches his head because of pain often. So I asked him

"You say son what happened that day."

The other kid and his parents were their too. My son said

"Papa (Father), that was our lunch period, he was sitting at the corner of a nearby bench, I got up from my seat, and somehow mistakenly his lunch box fell down, I said sorry, that was a mistake, but he started biting me and threw me on this table,"

I asked

"Is that kid around here? Can you recognize him?"

He said

"Yes papa, but, don't do anything that's okay, I am okay now."

This was something that other kid's parents were not knowing about and then something interesting happened.

His parents were shocked a little, and with the same shock, they asked their kid,

"What happened that day son?"

I don't agree with the social thought processes completely. But it was clearly visible they people were looking like they were not having formal enough education. Their clothing and accent were showing it a little. I didn't judge them for that. The answer of another kid was something which took my interest there, he said

"I was taking my lunch, and he made my lunch box fall down, so I had to teach him a lesson!"

The moment he said that, his father scolded him a little at that very moment, and said

"Son!, he must not have done that intentionally, this was wrong you shouldn't have done so, and said so, say sorry to him"

I was silent till then too, was just trying to observe everything that other kid said that, as if my kid did so intentionally, but this intention is not something we can find through communication. So of course I didn't make any judgment there. That kid said sorry to my son, my son was looking at me, I said

"Son, say sorry to him too, and say that that was a partial mistake of mine too, I will be more careful next time."

My son said the same, and even at the end of it, my son and that kid both were waving their hands at each other, with same pure feeling as if nothing happened a few minutes ago.

What I came to know is this support any deed, comes from the actual identity of the person. If a person gets support, this support also becomes the power, and so as capability too, and if the power is with him, somehow, supported any bad deed, then he not just continues to do so, he increases the intensity of doing every time he commits it. This happens as if it is a loop. Again and again kids face such situations, sometimes parents support them, and sometimes parents don't.

Now let's leave the term parents, and put intelligence, in place of this. If he has got power through intelligence. He starts using that power for his deeds. If these are good, it will be a ripple, if they are bad, will again be a ripple. Get ready for the worst then.

Now please compare everything that a mankind has made through intelligence. Let's take example of aero plane. Invention is made by either the wright brothers, or Shivakar bapuji Talpade, let the claim decide it by themselves, the thing is, they utilized their intelligence for the sake of good. Good happened, with this whole aero plane, the traveling has made tremendous growth. There is no question about that. We know the inventor's names because they utilized their capabilities towards their deeds of science. They believed in that identity only.

The people business owners now utilize it to earn through that as business, and use that as a transport system to serve humanity. That is their identity they utilized their capabilities for their identity.

But the same aero plane has been used to take down world trade centre 11th September 2001. The people who did this deed, they were also using their capabilities to do this deed. They utilized their intelligence, as well as, their team's intelligence, utilized whatever he has been given by others, the AK47, weapons, even an aero plane, they killed so many people. The most powerful line through their own capabilities they killed themselves. The question is, did the kill their identity? The answer is, they actually killed themselves for their identity.

So one thing is surely right here, almost everybody, the scientists, the terrorists, every doer, gives their complete capabilities to their identity. Whether they will exist or not. They tie themselves with their identity. Mostly it is often a name, their name, their' religion's name, their country's name, their community's name. They take everything like these as their identity. Is the name is an Identity?

"Remember that a person's name is to that person the sweetest and most important sound in any language."

- Dale Carnegie

You must be knowing about it, once a criminal do some big crime, he always try to find his name in the news, at least his bad deed. As he believes this is my identity. He utilizes all of his capabilities again in that bad deed. If he couldn't find his news in the pages, then he often try to hear his identity from at least some mouths. He even commits bigger crime to get his identity a priority, if gets the eye on page 7, now he attempts bigger to get on page 1. And this continues.

Suppose after murder he got caught by a policeman, this policeman also has his identity in his mind, his community, his nation, any role model, his honesty towards serving the nation, a good deed. But still his capabilities are devoted to his identity.

If the criminal has to appear in court. The judge's capabilities are going to serve his identity, he may either be crook, corrupt or honest. Good or bad deed he may do, but his capabilities are also being served to his identity.

If the criminal needs an advocate he also going to do the same. They say it's our primary responsibility to show the side of the clients of ours. And do our best to save our client. Even there is oath kind of things are there too.

If he got saved by the honest approach of the intelligent people what he may do after getting out to jail? Any guesses? He is going to do the same again because every feeling is related with their identity.

What I am trying to say is, the whole capabilities, whole intelligence, behaves overall as a servant to this identity. This identity in itself is everywhere but nowhere. This servant of identity is getting powerful day by day, if the owner of it is wrong, the whole intelligence becomes devil. If the identity is right, the intelligence becomes a god, almighty in itself. This is the power of identity one must understand. So if somebody says he is doing wrong or bad, it's not him, it's his believe over his identity.

Once I got chance to talk to an advocate sir, I met him in his office area, in court, the people as his clients were surrounding him. He is a friend of my father, I was listening the conversation of him with my father. His clients were looking like they aren't interested in education kind of thing at all. Their language, their body language, behaviour was not at all seeming good. As if they were bullies. When his client's left the office, my father asked him,
"Who were they brother?"
He said
"They all are bullies brother, dacoits, they all works to loot people, and looting people is their only business."
My father said
"Dealing with them is not a piece of cake brother, has to be hard"
He replied
"Harder then it seems brother, but what to say this is what our work is, and always has to be done"
I couldn't stop myself and I asked him
"Uncle, if you know they are bad people, then why are you saving him?"
He said

"Son, our duty is to present their side to the best, and to save them through that."
I said
"I may not be big enough to understand that, but still I was wondering, as we have been taught, if we do good, good comes back, and if we do bad, bad comes back."
He laughed a little and said
"Let me tell you a true story, once I was going out of city a little around only 45 kilometres around from here. Through my own bike, when I was on a highway, in the evening, I saw a delicate person asking for a lift, I thought he seems a good of a person, and I should be helping him, as it's getting darker, and he may get into trouble. So I stopped my bike there a little, just at the moment, when my bike stopped a little, 5 6 people, as dacoits, completely covering their face with some orange, red cloths, black cloths. They were running towards me, and were shouting on me, as 'STOP STOP STOP!, Let's take him' I came to know in an instance I am in big trouble now, I couldn't think of anything, but thought to run away from there, I tried to start my bike, but was sure, they may catch me, I started running through bike, and I heard a voice of one of the closest person of me, that voice was 'oh my god, advocate sir!'. I ran away from there, but the moment I was able to calm myself, I was pretty sure that person who recognized me has seen me from close. There are chances that he might be one of my client's here, as they all are also dacoits."
This story amazed me, for me it was like a hair rising experience. I asked with a strange face
"Don't you think uncle, they may have done something really bad to you, that could be really bad for your family too."
He agreed and said

"Yes you are right, that was a possibility"
I said
"If you know it, why are you doing this still? if there as somebody else, they could have robbed him or may have done something else to him, isn't it like trading, bad for bad"
He said
"Look son, it all is true, they are paying possibly from their robbery, from their bad deed, but I won't do that, there are more than 4000 advocates out there, if I won't do, they will, these robbers are going to be on road anyways. So weather I was there, or anybody else, it doesn't matter".

Do you really believe, that these should be saved? Who is right or who is wrong, we are not judge, and none of us is. But the result is a disaster. Who can be blamed for this? And this is one of the reason I really wanted to talk about it.

I really wish I could be completely agree with that statement advocate uncle. But I can't say that. Because I don't agree. This incident is overall an event of capabilities through different identities. But in between these there are many losses of normal life.

"When emotions dominate the intellect it leads to disaster and when intellect dominates then it harnesses the emotions."

- Gurudev Sri Sri Ravi Shankar

8:15am August 6, 1945, at Hiroshima, One atomic bomb named Little Boy has been dropped from Enola Gay.

And at Nagasaki, another bomb named Fat Man, was dropped from a Bockscar, at 11:02am, on August 9, 1945. It is a famous incident, almost everyone knows about it, 70,000 expected dead at Hiroshima, and 40000 is expected number of deaths at Nagasaki. Everybody knows about it. A dangerous example of use of Intelligence as power used to serve an Identity. Tried to attack another identity. Killed more than 110000 lives, this is counting of humans, which may be involved in that identity, individually were identities too. But uncountable the other creatures other animals insects, such died in this stunt of intelligence. And a nude dance of this weird aspect of intelligence its capabilities serving the identity without even thinking about it.

Adolf Hitler killed around 60, 00,000 people, utilized so many intelligent forces, and served logically a single identity, how in this world any use of such power is justified?

Let me ask you this, is this intelligence is the issue here? This intelligence has created something way powerful things than expected, say communication has made a huge growth, medical science has made a growth, not just that transport has made a huge growth too. So overall this intelligence of ours is not the problem. The question is very simple.

We can cut a tomato through a knife? Or we can kill somebody through it too? So is this knife is the problem? NOO! The problem is the one who is holding the knife.

Intelligence is as similar to this knife. The identity is the one who is holding it. This is the biggest issue here.

And what this identity is overall? It is a set of belief. Let's think it like this. A cloth is a cloth until we don't paint colours upon it. Orange colour above, green below, and white in between. Suddenly it is a flag, which was a cloth initially, it has become a feeling, and people are ready to die for that. This is a living example of identity. People die for it. I am not saying having love for your nation is bad. But if this love is killing something or somebody. It's not love, its obsession. In no good book, it is written as love is having anything with any bad deed.

Same thing is with cricket teams, football clubs, cities, streets, homes, religion, surnames, and each and everything which depicts identity now, has become something that everyone is following. We are attached with symbols too. It could even be the map of country, or map of world, set of lines, making any holy sign or anything. Overall if there is a good deed, which happens through the identity indeed a good thing it is. But if the bad deed is there too, then it has to be solved. We will be talking about good or bad later on too, but for now there is a solution of this misery.

The solution is we need a powerful wisdom, through which we can generate a powerful vision of our identity. And this is why the chapter 2 is wisdom, which started first and then the chapter one as identity. Because whatever we have with us, we may believe we may have generated through wisdom. But what we generated is a product of our intelligence which is going to serve our identity. So identity has to be decided at the very first. Which can be done through a very clear vision on identity, and this vision can be gained only and only through true wisdom. So if you believe you want to put the Identity chapter as 1st priority, I will respect your call, but the order to understand both is right here I believe. Anyways I want you to understand both. So will respect your decision anyways.

"Intelligence without wisdom brings destruction."

- Eron Ozan

The earth is 4.54 billion years old estimated age, The appearance of the oldest hominines may have been as early as 7 Million B.C.E.. Fossils suggests that humans are existing from 3,00,000 years. Before that there were no humans, which is less than 6% of earth's age. Evolution is here, this is how the whole universe is created, and everything and everyone is evolving. Question arise is, are we complete now? Or are we still evolving? Answer is clear we are still evolving, and this evolving means, there is still something may be incomplete within us, we are developing towards betterment right?

Even the word religion was formed around 16th 17th century, just 500 or 600 years ago. Even the word nation too was first used around 13th century. It is almost negligible in comparison the existence of earth.

The question arise is, who gave the right to give us identity to some human like creatures? To divide ourselves on the name of nation or religion or cast or anything. I am not against of any religion or nation. If they are for our good, definitely that could be a good thing to do, but if deaths blunders are happening coz of that, how can this even be supported.

Ask yourself, why this enlightment exist only 500 or 600 years back? if it is so, there are crores of creatures still out there who co exists with us, who are not following any religion or nation, few are on the border of nation, like a tree or plant, they aren't even aware of the situation that one day a grenade or bomb may take them down too. We have to think one more time, how are we any different from any of them. Or any of the creature in the world. What is our identity? And a humble request from me, let's not identify ourselves on any religious, nation, flag, culture, food, or anything such please. What is the bigger us inside us.

What I am willing to say is, this is the root cause of every destruction in the world, just a simple thing of thought that we are better and important than all the creatures in the world has made enough of damage to the world. On the name of nation one is killing the other and it is considered as right, on the name of religion same statement is true. We have to develop a wisdom which should be the primary focus of education too. This intelligence is so powerful that can serve the whole humanity, and this same thing is the one can destroy the whole humanity too. If wisdom is there than the intelligence can be in big control, as I believe intelligence just serves our identity. If the wisdom is there, build on pure knowledge of identity, I am pretty sure this intelligence can do no harm and will become a true power, and this what I believe the education can be of big help.

The reason for this identity is, we know everything because of the exposure. From the moment we take birth, we get exposure from everything and everyone. This exposure makes our mind set, knowledge and everything such. As an example we know this is a book, because somebody told this to us. Someone has already described it as the thing which you are holding right now is called a book. It is true with everything table, tree, or a cloth may be. Definitions of everything varies and changes from this exposure, every place has got a different language, or a different culture which decides for us. And this is where we need to know who we truly are. Because this is where the wisdom has to e built and this is where it may get spoiled.

Let's take an example of food, our exposure to the world takes us towards different food choices, most of the choices are from family from the beginning mainly, but it's not always true right? Initially parents are going to tell you what to eat what not to, than later, exposure increases, now pizza is there burger is there, fries, veg, non-veg, so many suggestions, from mobile, TV, friends, colleagues. Not just that this one is healthy and this one is not. This never ending battle in our mind won't stop until we won't end this. We have to make the final choice weather what to take what not to. This is true with every aspect in life too. Food is going to take place in a part of our body called stomach, now replace the food with thoughts, words, everyone is going to suggest it's their duty what is right what is wrong, so many thoughts so many mindsets, different choices but the final choice is what we have to hold. Just like the choice with the food is going to determine will we be healthier or not, similarly bad choice with the thoughts, and mindsets are going to decide our life. And if that's what going to decide our own one life only, that i wasn't going write this book. We live in a social world, and we are social animal, we are sharing the planet, somehow we are a part of that exposure too, if we are going to choose bad food often, we are going to create so many bad health mindsets around us often, same is true with the choice of words too. Take an example of anyone around you, a person bad health often gives opinions like, there is no harm in having a bite of pizza? Or any such bad health advice? Same is true with the smoker, there is a line.

"First cigarette or first peg of alcohol is always free"

Rahul Bajad

So I have got a personal reason of writing the book, you can take it in two ways.

1. You and I both are going to influence my family.
2. This whole world is my family.

Truthfully friend, you are my family. And so to change the exposure, we have to begin from ourselves. And to do so, we have to understand who we are actually. Knowing what we are and who we are is going to decide the whole world's wise future. And I want that to be best. We can both do this.

"We were born an Original, Why die a copy?"

- "John Mason"

I did write this one here, because, if we like something or if we feel pleasure in something towards it, we tend to take it inside us, the exposure we were talking about. We tend to duplicate ourselves with the ones we like by any means, often forgets to think about its good or not. Just like above I wrote somebody else's line here, thinking as if it's a good thing, and I will be able to give my point to you in a better way.

Take an example like this, if a leader of a country is corrupt, then the people tend to be corrupt too, most of them. If a family has got a culture of smoking, kids and youngsters tend to smoke often or earlier. See around you, we get everything from our company. There is nothing wrong with it if we are going to make the world a better place to live in that case, but if we are not able to use our wisdom towards it, we are going to make this world a worst place to live. So the exposure which gives us identity somehow, all I am trying to say is, if we could get proper wisdom on our identity too, we are not going to take everything as it is through the perspective of any identity being thrown at us. The whole world is live example of these weird duplications, cars are copy of each other, phones, chairs, homes, almost everything manmade are having essence of copy of one another. But I bet, we won't ever be able to find two trees who are copy of each other, two creatures exactly same, just like that we all are unique. With the true knowledge of what we are, I am pretty sure we will be way better.

"Everybody wants to rule the world"

- Earnest Cline

I am writing this one as, this is one of the weird most thought process I have seen in the world around us. The line is true for sure, and this is what we have got from the exposure of the world. It is not something that I am the only one who feels that they have seen around the world. Not just this, people don't just stop here. They even say the words like conquering the space. Let me ask you this, all the species of the world, are they sharing the earth or ruling the earth? We all are sharing the planet, it's of no one's but of everyone. Let me ask you another question, I am sharing two lines here, can you guess which line seems good?

"They is ruling the world"

"They are sharing the world"

Which of these two lines have got a feeling of love? The first one ruling the world means we and other people and creature have the surrender to them, as if they are above everyone, this is what the rule term means right?

In contrast the second statement has got the word "Share" with it, it mean that they are considering themselves as equal as the person who is reading this, or with everyone they are with, they considers themselves equal to them, definitely this statement has got no grudges.

And above this, is there any other creature on this planet who will ever think like this? The absolute answer is no. So why do we humans think as if we want to rule the world, and teach our kids that "Sharing is caring". This thought of being superior to others has done enough damage to the world. And from my perspective this is the main root of all the disaster of the world.

Imagine, there is a kind of disease which is spreading through air the whole city wasn't safe. Only an isolated school was one of the safe most place, the school was so big to take care of thousands of people. So almost 5000 people started staying there. Just because life wasn't possible for them out of school.

Almost they all settled in different rooms and halls in quantity of 100 200 500 depending on their own choices. Most of the room people usually don't prefer to talk often and remains silent loving all of them in fact serving the others like they used to cook food for others, work for others.

After some time leaders appeared, different thought processes appeared, few of the rooms have got people who were having some powerful mind-sets and they started having clashes with other room's leaders, which was obvious, every leader had followers and the more follower a leader had more powerful of a person he became.

Every leader was trying to protect and do well for their people, their room ones, their followers, they started making some strategies which they thought should be helpful for the growth of their people. Like making a crossway path from one room to another the middle rooms aren't required. The people who were following the those leader were in profit, got more space and easy to serve them, those who were not following were having couple of disputes with those leaders but again the powerful leader who had most followers were ruling that place too.

But the people who were serving all of them, lost their shelters as they were living in between those rooms which were coming in the middle of path, battles were there because of disagreements, somebody was saying this place is mine, someone else was quarrelling as this place belong to him, those were fighting someone was dying. Those who were not saying anything, were silent from the beginning were getting killed by the leaders. Soon out of those 5000 only the 100 people killed almost 2500 of people, and rest were all only following these.

I was having one simple question through this story. Who is the villain?

Can't they all could have lived peacefully serving each other's?

The whole school got destroyed on the name of those 100 people who believed they are the leaders of the whole school, and they are working for the benefit of their own people.

Suppose I make you judge here, and would say that you have right to do anything, will you give punishment to somebody? For this?

If you will give punishment to somebody who will be those?

What punishment would that be?

Let me present the exact perspective I am trying to tell you. Let me introduce the exact words what I was trying to tell you. The School is our mother earth. Out of the school we can't survive no one can. Do you know who those 100 people are? Its humans, who believe they are ruling the world and deserve to rule the world.

Trees are the ones who are serving the whole humanity this air oxygen is something they are giving us all the time. And we are killing them almost all the time for our benefit. Not just them, the horse, the bulls, cows, buffalos, and fishes we are harming them all, all the time, for the sake of betterment of humans? Seriously? Suppose we think to create a bridge, loss of old trees and plants are going to cut, just because of our betterment, suppose we need a land and need to make a home for us, we cut more than 1000's of species down kill so many lives or send them somewhere else just to make it better life for couple of humans? Is this fair? Is this what sharing is all about?

If somebody kills somebody than we have got a death sentence for that person. But if he or she is the person. If it's an animal, or a tree or a plant, or a fish. What rubbish I am talking here right? Is this what sharing is all about? I know there is one big misunderstanding lives in between that we have to kill for survival.

The answer is a big no. what I am willing to tell you is, take an example of a forest. A lion is more powerful than a human, powerful enough to take care of almost every animal over there, but does he ever try to take down every animal in one day? Or just one for the food? Does he ever think for the future generations? Or even for tomorrow? It's a big NO. He only thinks for today, and lives like a King. If he would have thought like us, than he may have killed everyone in the forest for his future. Just like humans, we need for tomorrow, we need for day after that and after that and so on. Not just that when a lion kills somebody for his own food. Before the death of that animal the animal was living freely in the world. The animal was going to be the food of lion but he didn't lived his life under a cage worrying I am going to be killed by lion for the food one day?

But humans, just one thought that we are superior to others, we make chickens suffer till the end of their last breath just because we are going to eat them one day. Suppose if the chickens will become human and humans become chickens than? If they will eat us and put we in cage till the end of our last breath just because they eats us. We suddenly would think this is bad, this is not something should be happening. But that would be justice.

All I am trying to say is, we can't change what has happened already, but we can now. At least we can try now. Let's know the true meaning of humans, let's know the true meaning of our identity. Let's consider ourselves as if we are sharing the whole planet. Not just an owner of a home, or a citizen of a state or country. We are not superior but all is our family. It's not that I am the only one who is concerned about it. So many life cycles are getting disturbed by our weirder behaviour. And so many people and creature who are looking for justice are waiting for the day when this line would come true.

"Nature has got the tendency to balance itself"

- Anonymous

-

There is one more word in the world which is very common and creates so much misunderstandings too about it, people tend to believe their identity according to it. And term is very controversial too. The word name is "Religion"

I bet if you could find one proper definition of this word Religion anywhere, or on the internet too. Just because there is none.

I am not in against of any religion or identity, but I am pretty sure for one thing that no religion can ever teach us killing, or superiority or disrespectfulness. So if a religion is not teaching us those we should get close towards the purpose of it.

"The purpose of religion is to control yourself not to criticize others."

- Dalai Lama

Again I am not comparing any religion here, but what I am trying to convey the true and the most important meaning here is our identity. What we should know before we get to use our intelligence. Through any mean.

Let's try to understand the concept of religion through a story.

What happened was once few scientists were trying to understand the behaviour of monkeys through an experiment. What they did is, they made a big cage and kept say 10 monkeys inside of it. In that cage above it, they made a ladder and hanged a set of bananas above it. What they used to do is, whenever if any one of the monkey tries to get to the bananas they make artificial rain and that wets every monkey in the cage. They did the same thing for couple of times, whenever any of the monkey tries to get the bananas, they wet all the monkey, after a while they noticed one thing. That the monkeys were now afraid of this situation, but they were wanting banana too.

After some tries when they came to know that whenever someone tries to get banana the rain happens, so they stopped trying, but if anyone did the same thing and tried to get the banana, the other 9 monkeys were pulling the leg and were stopping the one monkey if the monkey still tries to get the banana they even bit the monkey too. After some time all monkeys were set, and were knowing no one can get the bananas, if anyone tries so, they will get beat and rain will happen too.

After some time they replaced 1 monkey out of 10 monkeys and this new monkey was not knowing about what to be done and was willing to get the banana but when he tries so, all the other 9 monkeys stopped him and bit him too, he was very much confused what should I be doing, what wrong am I doing, why these other monkeys are beating me. But after 2 3 small fights the new monkey gives up on it.

Then after some time they replace another, same thing happened this new monkey too, but this time 8 were beating one was watching and the new one was getting beaten without knowing the reason. Why they are not taking down the banana. And not let me take that too.

They did same thing again, after a while the no monkey was old in the cage, all the monkeys were new, now rain isn't there, banana is there, but they all were knowing if any monkey will try to catch the banana. The others are going to beat them.

This whole story best explains the belief, just like the old monkeys were believing something new monkeys doesn't have to, if the new monkeys won't follow it old monkeys won't be happy. But this doesn't necessarily mean the old monkeys are right or the new monkeys are wrong. Or vice versa this doesn't necessarily mean that the new monkey are right or the old ones are wrong.

I mean look at the whole evolution and discoveries, initially earth was flat, than later it became round. Sun used to revolve our earth, than later earth started revolving. Every belief has a reason.

"When the why is clear, How is easy"

- Anonymous

I am not saying that old belief is good or the new one. I am just trying to say is at least we should be asking questions "WHY?" or we can try to find out answer at least by ourselves or something before believing in anything wrong or right. Especially when it is about our identity what we are and who we are.

And I really believe that no religion stops questions. Every religion welcomes it.

Asking questions is mandatory from my perspective, this sign indicates a lot, if a student's ask questions this mean that he is trying to understand or has got a doubt on something. But when we get old we stops this habit, main reason could be anything, even our elders tries to push something on us, or our boss, or our senior I am not saying to disrespect them, but the least we could do is, if we have questions specially regarding to something which may affect the life of our family or our surroundings, we should try to find answers.

The reason it is necessary is that, if we won't be able to find our true identity, then people are going to misuse it, if we won't ask questions people are going to take advantage of it, they are going to justify your identity and your thoughts in their favour.

The biggest example of this is something we can get from some movies, I am not saying that having love for our nation is bad, but we shouldn't be very blind at it, we shouldn't forget what we are above nation too.

Every country has got some movies which are very famous and great too, which are having love for their nation amazing thought process, but they will show the neighbour country as the villain, that the country near us is trying to capture us, is trying to bully us, and they represent themselves as bad people, and some soldiers who are dying for our country is the hero, off course a person who is willing to do something really good for the country is a hero. But i am against of the representation is evil and hero. To make the hero a bigger hero, they are trying to prove that the villain is really bad. There is a line that

"A person can't be that ugly as shown in the government id, and can't be that beautiful either as shown in the social media profile"

- Anonymous

I agree both kinds of people exist in world good and bad, but half-truth is half lie too. There are thousands of things as example you can get if you will just look around you, we born as human in the world, than later we get a name, our name decides our religion, our birth and family decides our beliefs, our birth place decides our nationality, and so on. Suppose the same person may have born in any other country than the nationality could be different now he may be willing to die for different country?

Life won't stop just here, not just our parents or our family, people around us also puts so many things in our mind, things around us are being used to manipulate us.

"We become what we think about most of the time, and that's the strangest secret"

- Earl Nightingale

-

Say, a movie star, is looking cool and hard, he drinks and he smokes, now the generation automatically thinks that smoking is cool, drinking is awesome, not just because they know how this is going to effect, but just because that celebrity is doing kids follow them, bad truth follow these blindly. If the movie star is university topper no one is going to copy that, If the movie star spends 1 hour daily in gym for physical fitness, almost no one is going to do that, if the movie star is very humble and good, almost no one is going to do that, if the movie star is really trying to do something amazing and good in that movie, almost no one is going to do that, but if he smokes, so many are going to do the same, in the same way too, if he drinks so many are going to do that in the same manner. And people take advantage of this weird habit of ours.

"We first make our habits, and then our habits makes us."

- John Dryden

As I am saying again and again, we have to develop a powerful wisdom to understand, that manipulation will always be there, we have to make ourselves wise enough to know what we are, than only we will be able to do good around.

Else being a part of bad, is a big bad itself.

In case of these powerful manipulation. Take example of festivals, in India it is quite common during festivals television advertises YouTube advertises, and social media advertises of chocolates increases, a try of influence, that the best gift to give your loved one is chocolate, if it's a family than Diwali gift, if it's a raakhi, Christmas or any of the holy or festivals, than best gift is chocolate for sister, for family, if it is a valentine day, than again it is the best gift to give a chocolate it suddenly becomes the symbol of love. And people starts following it. Not just those, celebrities promotes these.

Vice versa, at the time of festivals local market things will automatically get criticized, example during the time or raakhi, regional sweets any video becomes viral saying there are so many bad things in the regional sweets, and this happens only around Diwali, raakhi or any festivals, it is true for whole of the world.

Were the bad mixtures of things weren't available in the regional sweets before, yes there was, but that thing won't be highlighted until the festival comes. Not just that are you 100% sure, that the chocolates are as good as how they represent it, there are cases available in court about these too, but those court cases about the quality will never ever come in media, or social media or any of the platform, these will never get viral, do you know the reason? This is how they play with our mind. For the sake of profit.

Take another example of some cold drinks available in market, try to see their commercials, if they don't have any of the ingredient to talk about as quality, they will try to make it a status symbol just like chocolates, they will relate it to youth, style symbol, that if you will drink cold drink you will look cool. And if there is a health issue with someone and somebody complains about it, that complain will never ever get public, they will pay crores of bucks to shut that thing out of media. But the worst thing is we don't take it seriously.

Things not just stop here, our cell phones, try to search anything, you will instantly see advertises related to your search, as if they are keeping eye on us. This is also a manipulation.

Imagine like this, the best place to give treat to our friends and family is a pizza place, so let's eat pizza, the best drink to drink is a cold drink or alcohol, let's drink them, the chocolates are the best way to be happy, let's eat them too, ask yourself If we do so daily are we making a good life or a bad life for us as well as for our kids too?

I want you to answer yourself, a pizza is better or homemade chapattis? A burger is better or some cooked vegetables at home, a cold drink is better or a lemon juice made at home, take any example, health is better at sleeping on some mattresses or a met like the old times where our spine will be straight, a costly toothpaste is better or a neem (Indian lilac) stick?

My father once asked me that my stomach is not good, I am not feeling well from couple of days, so I have ordered from a friends suggestions these two capsules of Indian Lilac and turmeric capsules these have got pure of these, and very healthy for us.

I asked him directly, we have got turmeric at our home, and Indian lilac tree just outside of it, which is fresh too, why don't you take it directly?

Even I laugh sometimes that some Ayurvedic products has got advertises like this rare herb is 1000's of years old very unique and very powerful ingredient of our product, very much beneficial for us, and the same product has got expiry of 6 months. Are you seriously buying this?

If we and our kids will become wise and will have some powerful wisdom, and I am more than sure, they will be better humans and better human make a good world around himself and for the world too.

"Human beings are social animals, we were social before we were humans"

- Peter Singer

Even if the line was said by somebody else too, then also the line was true, we are actually social animals, and I want you to be with the happiest company possible. Writing this one just because you should be knowing that there are people who are misusing and misleading us, for their profit. Take this as an example.

It is not very uncommon, that we are in a group sitting with each other, but instead of sharing thoughts and discussion with each other, most of the time we are with somebody else, sharing the pictures of food, the restaurant's place pictures, even selfies of nobody else just alone of us. I am not against of happiness, but it should be from inside as far as I believe. Likes comments and subscribes can't be our identity, taking a selfie alone is one of the example of being unsocial. We are learning this from around us, which is not that trustworthy.

Overall I am trying to say, this has made enough of harms to the generations already, using the technology is a good thing, getting used by technology is a blunder.

"I fear the day when the technology overlaps with our humanity. The world will only have a generation of idiots."

- Albert Einstein

I mean come on, we want to go out for fun, people want to go for a movie, One screen overall in a dark hall which has nothing but screen visible, off course with some advertises, if we want to go work, we are going to do this on a screen, if we want to talk to our relatives, we are again using screens to interact, if we are overseas, if we are in different city, even if we are in the same building too. If we have some free time, even if we are sitting in public, let's scroll some reels, or let's nudge a friend on chat or something. If there is a family entertainment, let's go watch television, or any OTT, don't you think almost everything has come on screens, not with the real life people? If it is something we were wanting, or our identity is, than off course go for it, but if it is something what you actually want? But if it is something that owner of any social media is wanting you to do, or the owner of a cell phone company is wanting you to do, or an operating system maker is wanting you to do, then it's their wish, we might be just draining ourselves for their wish and happiness.

And I am not just throwing stones, a famous social media company owner accepted the fact that he puts a cello tape on the camera of his screens, a world famous mobile phone company owner accepted that his own kids are not allowed to use the gadgets of his own.

My question is very simple, if I have made a juice and it is healthy, the very first thing I would want that to benefit me and my family, my loved ones, but if it is not healthy whatever I have made, then? I won't let my loved ones drink that.

I read that too, a famous restaurant owner, also made a statement, that he himself doesn't take burger of his own, and neither let his own family take so. Cold drinks are also a good example, they don't let their own family people drink that, but a celebrity is definitely going to come to your screen and going to say that it is a good thing, I am drinking it.

Ask yourself, will any celebrity would want their kids to smoke? The answer is simple, but they are endorsing those cigarettes, which is not something made to be endorsed.

Willing to say is, let's explore ourselves, what we are, try to find out what do you actually want, not through social media, that you want that car, or that bike or that home, that way you are going to work for whole of your life for that car company owner, or some real estate or bank for whole of our life, if we make our decision wrong about what do we actually want or what do we actually want to become. And your true dream will get washed away by a fake wish which has been influenced upon you, intentionally for their own profit. That what we have to decide whether to be a puppet of theirs, or a free bird.

It is not something our mind make up is something which is being tried now, from years and years, this is happening and some are worst of the doings of the greedy people, who somehow killed the free powerful souls of us. Let me tell you about another example. You might have heard the demonetization, but have you heard the word demoralization?

"Demoralization of the target audience is yet another step in powerful mind control."

- Joost Meerlo

In India when some people were trying to capture the India, they sent some intelligent people to find out how to capture the India, they stayed in India for years, and with a powerful study, they came on a conclusion, they have to destroy the backbone as of India, as the gurukuls of India, and to do so they made strategy to manipulate India from their own cultures, they took some dumb people in India, took them to abroad convinced them that their culture is better than Indian culture, through appreciation, and proper planning they planted themselves in different parts of the India, And it has been done intentionally, and slowly Indians stopped loving their own culture. How did they do that?

Do you remember there were some high earning movies, were in trend in India, where the villain of the movie is usually a pandit or priest, or a big Indian guru, or somebody who worships god often, and such, there are plenty of movies which somehow put the people who are villain and are somehow religious. Our younger generation got a little distracted and away from religious beliefs. This is just an example so many slogans are there, which are still with the TV commercials too. Which somehow leads to some misbeliefs to play with the identity, I am not saying that we may have some spiritual identities, I want you to find out by your own, decide by your own. Proofs being

There were almost 7,32,000 Gurukuls were there in India during 5000BC, and at the time of 2022 there were almost 4500+ remained only, not just that out of which 2912 are struggling to survive. It's not like they don't have quality education. They have got very powerful proved techniques of education but the priority has been shifted to something else in India too.

Let me ask you this, suppose if I would give you a burger, a chapatti, a poison fruit, a piece of garbage from dustbin, a chalk, a piece of soil, and a paper piece. What would you choose to eat? Either the tastier one, or which would be beneficial for us right? We take only those thing inside our body which are good for us, not those things which are bad for us. Why don't we do the same for thoughts as well?

Whatever we see somehow makes an impression on mind, whatever we hear makes an impression, our senses are almost fully responsible for everything we are letting to get inside of us, we differentiate this with our eating priorities, but why don't we do the same for what we see? Or what we hear? I get it that whatever we are having in our surroundings we learn a lot from those, and this is what I believe too, we should learn from it, but if someone else is wanting us to learn for their profit, we should have enough wisdom what to take what not to take inside.

"Clean and nourish your mind wisely every day. It can easily become a garbage bin."

- Philip Arnold

I see so many homes, where there are so many soap operas are famous, I was observing one girl saying while watching the television, if my mother in law will do anything like this, I will show her no mercy, don't you think this thought, even before the age of getting married, is going to create chaos in her life, the impression of this thought and side effect is definitely going to create a kind of mind-set that mother in law is a bad person and might do something bad, and the girl after marriage is going to find bad in her mother in law for sure, no matter how hard her mother in law will try to be good in front of her, the good deed will be wasted, and sooner or later, the mother in law may make a mistake, off course there will be, no one's god, everybody has right to make mistake, that's how we can prove that we are humans. Soap opera people are going to earn a lot of money through this, but the identity impression what they are creating to the child's brain is going to be really dangerous. This is an example of the garbage is being put in the brain.

Let me ask you this, suppose you need 50k bucks right here right now? Who can give you this amount right now? You might be thinking about some of the people around you, your closed one or your nearby, may be your loved ones, let me get this straight to you, first condition is, the person should have 50k bucks to give you, right? And the person who has 50k is the only one who can give too? Isn't this philosophy same for everyone and everything. If a person has got something good, that person can give something good, whether it's a plant, money, a ball, a toy or may be thought. But what if the person has nothing but garbage inside him or her. Now he can only give garbage as that's all he has.

Look around you, a positive person always gives positive thoughts and spreads positivity, vice versa a negative person spreads the same negativity. A person who is energizing, spreads energy around him, vice versa is also true, a person who has got nothing but tiredness with him, spreads the same around him. Take the example of that girl above, who has got this weird bad thought about the future mother in law, what she is going to do, now she is going to spread the same garbage around her, in the minds of her friends. This is what we do from our birth, if we like anything we recommend it, to our loved ones, that's how the culture of forwarding in any social media has took birth. The easiest way to spread the amazingness of life, the positivity and vice versa the easiest way to spread the garbage, bad videos, bad thoughts, and everything else too which will get into our mind knowingly unknowingly.

Can you even imagine how this thing can be a disaster?

"You become what you surround yourself with. Energies are contagious. Choose carefully. Your environment will become you."

- Anonymous

I was reading about the study of a person who was in sleep, scientists were having a kind of experiment on his body, when he was in deep sleep, they were continuously putting in his mind that, now we are going to put a piping hot, red iron rod on your hand, your hand will burn. And when the scientists did so, his hand burned up from that rod, with clear visibility of blisters on his hand. You might be thinking what's new in this. The rod was cold not hot, it was his own mind who burned his own body, without any external heat. It's not the thing I want you to take from here, the scientists made the reverse experiment too on him, and he did heal himself with those burnt hand, his had become normal again, as if nothing such happened, blisters were also gone. This was an experiment about which you can find the same in the book called power of happy thoughts.

If this is true, can you even imagine, how much it is necessary to not let any bad or garbage thought into our mind by anybody? Scientists have got proof that the mind has got the power to heal our body from almost anything. But healing ourselves needs good thoughts right? What if we don't have space for good thoughts to heal ourselves?

Take another example of Covid times, Everybody was continuously sharing almost everything through social media, how many people are dying every day, people were sharing the number of deaths daily, almost no one was sharing how many people got recovered every day, but how many are dying every day. Everybody was worried of death, at that critical situation scientists made vaccines we don't how hard that work could be, but social media and media was continuously criticizing those vaccines. The pictures of deadly disasters were being sold all over. Will vaccine be helpful or it may kill us, who to trust who not to, our people, loved ones, everyone was afraid. How many of us were able to remain positive and were able to keep good thoughts in our mind.

For the very first time I heard that court ordered a media person that she doesn't have any more rights to talk or write on vaccine, just because she was telling half-truths and misleading people. But that news didn't have viral that she spread, half-truth, and mislead people. Only misleads about her bad articles, bad pictures took place inside of so many people.

It's not the first time media was doing so, social media, television media, news media, newspapers, almost everyone is working for money, almost no one was even concerned that how this news or half lie is going to affect most of the people. But it's not just them, we barely think what is getting inside of us in thoughts, and we barely worry about the side effects of these thoughts into us. And even we keep on sharing the same, thinking as if we are helping the ones we care about. But are we actually going to give some good positive effect of what we are sharing with our loved ones or this is going to create another bad effect on them.

Now imagine like this, suppose the people around the globe, the media people, the social media owners, the television people, every one decides just for once, that we are good people, and lives are way prior than money, and they decides that we will only show good things which could give good effect on the mindset on people, isn't there content about good efforts on Covid people. The people Sonu Sood was doing, the doctors who were working day and night to save us all, the rich people who were feeding thousands of people, the good people who are serving the groceries and milk products door to door, risking their own lives, the people who are transferring medicines masks, who doesn't have to wait for the picture of any big politicians, the powerful good religious people, who doesn't care about what religion the person is of, but they were trying their best to help in need of. The people who were not at all coming in media. Just because a bad and critical news is saleable, and a good news is not going to make them a fortune.

May the eternal power would give them enough wisdom to make the life more important than money in their mind, but before that we have got the power to change our priorities and thoughts, we can develop a strong wisdom on the acts what we do what we share, is this is something which is going to make good effect or is not going to make one. Or at the least we can isolate ourselves from something which we don't want in the world to happen again.

"What you think, you become, what you feel you attract, what you imagine you create"

- Buddha.

Once my son was ill, having fever, I took him to our family doctor, he was quite young at that age might be 2 years something he was able to speak or talk that also no much. After couple of months he again got fever, I took him to our family doctor again. We went to him, He saw my son, put his hand near the throat, he checked his hand, asked some simple questions, and said

"He has got a little fever",

He gave the pills and put both of his hands around the cheeks of my son, gave him a small chocolate, and told him,

"You will be doing great by tomorrow and will again start riding on your bicycle."

The process was almost something that twice a year, I have to take him to the doctor. Once he again got fever at the age of 7, he said

"Papa I want to go to our family doctor."

But I was out of town, so seeing him wasn't that easy, so I tried to have him convinced that

"Let's go and see another doctor son"

He said

"No I want to see our family doctor only."

We weren't that far, so I took him back to the city and took him to the same family doctor of ours, I was a little afraid that what may have happened to my kid, the doctor saw him, again gave some pills, he is a homeopathic doctor, so almost all the pills look similar, We went to him, He saw my son, put his hand near the throat, he checked his hand, asked some simple questions, and said

"He has got a little fever",

He gave the pills and put both of his hands around the cheeks of my son, gave him a small chocolate, and told him,

"You will be doing great by tomorrow and will again start riding on your bicycle."

I couldn't resist to ask now, my wife took my son, and I got back to doctor again, with a little curiosity,

"Sir do you know black magic or something, how is this possible that in a day, he always loses his fever, and you solve it with one or two pills all the time",

He smiled and said

"Yes I know the black magic."

I was smiling too, but with curiosity,

"I mean it, I want to know."

As I was coming to him from years, he said,

"Your son was almost never ill sir",

He hardly gets a fever, now I was more curious,

"What the! What! What are you talking about".

He smiled and said,

"Have you heard the name Placebo?"

I said

"A little, maybe"

Then he explained

"Placebo is a powerful effect that happens within our body, just by believing that, we are taking a pill from a doctor we trust, and we will be fine soon, through this treatment. The body heals itself, through this belief, he just have got this belief in me, and in my treatment, and your wife got that too in me"

That was shocking a little for me

"Do you mean my wife isn't sick with asthma either?"

She used to take treatment from him from

years for her asthma, he said

"She does have, but not up to what she expect she has"
I asked

"This explains a little but that what about these pills than, isn't these harmful in that case? I mean if the body is healing themselves, then the medication is harmful, right?"

He laughed out a little more, and in front of me, he took couple of those pills in mouth and offered me the same,

"You can take these too?"

I said with so many pauses and confusion too,

"Thank you, for the offering, but not getting it"

He smiled and said

“These are just sugar pills, nothing else than sugar in your son’s case, and in your wife’s most of the cases”

“I almost never gave your son a medicine. Most of the time it’s just sugar pills, your son believes that I went to the doctor, in the whole process from coming here, to the moment he is going back to home, until he starts riding his bicycle, he continuously reminds himself that I went to the doctor, he has seen me, he gave me the medicine, I am taking the medicine, and I will be amazing and will be riding my bicycle tomorrow, his belief heals himself, this whole effect is called placebo effect” So lastly I asked him,

“If a positive thought can heal us, than a negative thought could it create the same issues with the body?”

He said

“In certain cases it is true, just like the case of your wife, she is generating asthma in her body, and then she comes to me, and solves that issue mostly by herself, it’s like fighting with ourselves and winning again from ourselves, and the moment you will tell them the truth, this whole effect will stop working, and they may get ill again, that’s why I didn’t tell you previously and almost we don’t tell this to anyone, and almost nobody asks like this either, so try not to let them know”

That was mind opening, so I tried that myself, when I was going out of the city, I took a bottle of sugar pills, and made a video call with the sir, and he said to my son

“Son, I gave your father, a powerful pill for every issue with your body, whenever you feel ill, you can ask your father, and take them, but they are very powerful don't take more than two once, Okay?"

My son was so happy hearing so, and said

"Now, I can go on vacation without any doubts, I am free, thank you sir!, thank you papa!"

After a while, my son came to me, papa I am not feeling good, do you have got those pills, now I touched his hand, his throat, used even that thermometer, even I he is okay, I says

"hmmm, you are just a little ill, take these pills, but only two they are powerful, after that, I put both of my hands around his cheeks and said, you will be doing amazing son, tomorrow you are going to ride your bicycle again"

And this process is still being followed, now he is 9 years young, my son hasn't seen hospital till now from inside, that how the hospital actually looks like.

So let's get a solution oriented approach here, through this story what I am trying to tell you is, if a good thought and positive thought about ourselves can heal us and can show some magical effect on us. Can't it create some negative effects on ourselves? That's the reason I was trying to tell you that, we have to keep a guard around our mind and thoughts that no one around us no person, no media no social media should put a bad thought about anything into our mind, as the bad thought has got some powerful side effect of it too. For this we have to build a strong very strong wisdom, we have to know ourselves how things are going to work around us. Or a clear idea of at least ourselves. In case of placebo, know the effect of it can reverse its effect too, but if we can develop a powerful wisdom, I am pretty sure we can have and become the best possible of us too for sure.

"I assure you, an educated fool is more foolish than an uneducated one."

- Moliere

Once a person gets this weird idea into his own mind, that I am better, the moment he begins thinking like this. He has become a disaster now. From the beginning of evolution, we all are continuously evolving, every opinion changes with time, there were so many theories later proved wrong my friend. Having an ego of our knowledge, and having knowledge of our ego. These both are contrasting statements. But so true, I shared in the beginning as well, we are right will not ever mean the person in front of us is wrong. If you remember that hidden pencil in the pocket of kid.

Once I got to learn a powerful thing from a one of the powerful teacher I have ever met, and I respect him a lot. He was trying to teach a similar concept there he mentioned that, "I see so many people, who are graduate, completes their masters, even they do certain PhD's too, more they get educated, more egoistic they starts to become, the start calling themselves as I am a professor, I know this I know that, but knowledge is a very tricky thing, every subject in the whole world is as vast as like sea, and no matter how hard we try, we can maximum capture a glass of water from that sea in comparison of that knowledge, definitely that knowledge can be more than most of the people, but it will never be enough, so having proud on one glass of water in front of whole of the sea is disgusting thought process, the sea in front, never says a thing, it holds whales, sharks, and a small fish can't even live in that glass, this could be a hypothetical approach, but he said, a person with true education, is knowing that sea is in front, there is a lot more to know, and what I still know very minute, he will never be content of knowledge, this thrust of knowledge will never end for him, and this will make him only a student, never a professor, a person with true education, should always be as humble as a person who accepts he knows nothing.

My father used to say too, a tree full of fruits will always bent over. This too should be the purpose of education, and it should be one of the destiny of it.

"Beauty begins the moment you decide to be yourself"

- Coco chanel

There are two types of things in the world, one is manmade, and another one is not man made. Every species in the world, ancient good books were saying there are something 84 lakhs of species, scientists might commit that there could be something around 1cr or more of the species around the globe. But I am pretty sure about the specie name humans. We are the only specie who has got wisdom or has got enough of presence of active mind to develop a powerful wisdom for sure. Initially we were very much focused on what is not man made, and we were respecting that to. Like nature, there was a kind of thought process that we are sharing the planet. Than later that we are the only creature who has powerful mind. We started believing we don't share the world. We can rule the world, even some idiotic lines are available on google that we can conquer the space or universe too. But still the truth is we are sharing the planet. The only thought that we are way better than every other creature of this world has done enough of the damage to the world. But if we somehow can develop a powerful true wisdom, than we can know that we are sharing the planet. Sharing the world. Everyone has got equal right on everything.

The world exists from millions billions of years, humans exist only from like a 3,00,000 years, and all these religions are almost just 500 years old at max. I was wanting you to identify yourself from what is not man made at least. We used to respect nature and every being. Now the world has become business, Education has become business, Medical industry is an industry now, Hospitality is an industry now, and most of the people are putting man made things ahead of man or any of the world's creatures itself.

Suddenly mangoes are not something parrots can eat without the permission of mango tree owner, suddenly animals have to leave the forest just because a 5 star hotel is going to come at the place where they used to live, trees have to sacrifice their lives, just because humans think they own the land, and just like the ashes of the tree, one day everything and everyone will become the ash. So taking the life of the tree for the sake of land doesn't actually makes much sense. My words may sound a little weird to you here.

But think like this, the whole dilemma of the world has come to a place where our kids are going to learn that we worship trees and on the other side we cut them for a piece of land. Which is not explainable completely. A little Hippocratic thought. At one place we worship animals and on the other hand we give them a miserable life that one day we have to eat them, so they have to live in a cage for forever till we don't cut them in parts. And the people who do so, call it their living. Technically they may be right, think like this a lion also eats an animal, but the moment lion takes life of an animal, that animal was having a freedom, and has lived his life with his family or at least may have spent some happy moments bad moments in his life, and then the lion takes his life, not for money, to actually fulfill his hungry desires, and we can call it living too, but after that one hunt, the whole of the forest feels safe from him, until his next hunger. That's how the nature has balanced himself. But humans on the other side wants to have food for today, if they have for today, now they want for tomorrow, if they have got sufficient for tomorrow, now they want for the week, than a month, than of a year, than a decade, then for his whole life, if he has got enough for his life, now he wants to earn for his children's life, if he has got enough for the children's life, now he wants to earn for hi next future generations, his grandson, and so on and so on. He never stops. He is like a lion who can take anyone's life anytime he wants for food off course but killing everyone around him, and puts them in refrigerator for his grandson's too. I am not judge here, but ask yourself, do you want your kids to be something like this? Or you want them to become something amazing who could be better than us at least?

So, I am more than sure about one thing, that the education should not be something that somehow corrupts our identity with something which we are not, or something we may not want to become, but at least about the true identity of ourselves, we can be the most beautiful creature of the world, if we start believing we are sharing the planet, we are a life, just like others. But if I am going to tell you this, than this will also be a kind of pre made thought process, which could give you an identity. Which I don't want to do, I want you be the best beautiful of you and same for our kids. I believe education should not be something that is going to tell them how to increase the number in their bank account. It should be way more than that, this can be done if we can be the best beautiful creatures of the world.

There was a line that, may be, education can be bought from school, but wisdom is something you can't. And there are plenty of the things which can't be learned from the school's education, you know in Germany the education system is dual one, both academic learning and practical training. Students alternate between studying theory at a vocational school and gaining practical work experience. This practical approach towards education lets them explore themselves more, develops more of the wisdom and they could develop their own learning and identity.

The moment we will get closer to the true identity of ourselves, I am more than sure we will be able to find more peace, more beauty, and more life, let's make our kids the most beautiful life on planet. Not an owner of a greedy mind, who's a money making machine, but a beautiful heart. And be the best life possible in the world.

"A beautiful heart will bring things into your life that all the money in the world couldn't get you."

- Karen Salmansohn

There are plenty of things which has already decided about the identity of yours, from your birth

- Your religion

- Your name
- Your family
- Your nation
- Your culture
- Your food values
- Your cloths priorities
- Your rights mostly
- Your wrongs mostly
- Your laws to be followed
- Your possibilities mostly.

And so many, good or bad you decide with your own wisdom. I want you to have one powerful wisdom, and I am sure your will be able to develop that.

From my perspective, it doesn't matter where we born, we all have to one unit to be the best of us. So to make it simpler you and I both got birth on same planet, sharing the same planet, almost very similar life we have. I really wish that you will be able to explore the best possible unique identity of yours. And have an amazing life ahead.

"The best possible wisdom can only be gained once you will discover your true identity."

\- Rahul Bajad

Necessity 3

Purpose

"The purpose of education is to replace an empty mind with an open one."

Malcom S. Forbes

There is a reason behind everything, and everything happens for a reason. What if the reason for doing something isn't worth it?

My son asked his grandfather very innocently

"Daadu, why should I study in school?"

Daadu replied

"Because you have to be capable enough to earn your living son."

He couldn't understand this one, so he asked the same question to his Daadi

(Grand Mother)? Daadi said

"If you will not study son, you will not get good girl to marry."

He didn't understand this either so he asked his mother

"Mummy can you answer me why should I study?"

She replied

“Son, to become successful, you have to study”

It still was not the satisfying answer either for him, he was and he is still looking for the answer of the Question, do you know the answer?

To be a better person?

To be a better employee?

To get a good job?

To be successful?

Or for the preparation of better future,

There are 100’s of answers available on the google too if you will search this?

This is where everything lies, and this is where so many lies exist too. When a kid gets to school for the very the first time, what could be the possible reason a 5 6 or 8 years young kid may have in his mind? Any of the above? No chance. He likes to play, he likes to be happy, and he is exploring the whole world.

"What makes a child gifted and talented may not always be good grades in school, but a different way of looking at the world and learning."

- Chuck Grassley

While I was in the process of selecting the very first school for my kid. I was thinking as if I was the most unique and most caring father in the world. I started visiting so many schools. What was I looking for, the best place for my kid, safety and love being the first priority, and off course, education was not my priority initially. But let's be honest this feelings always had a small place in mind. That's the reason at the age of 2 and a half year I got to the school just like so many parents, although this was a kid's pre-primary school. But back in mind a thought exists that if I will be able to get my kids admission earlier in this age, he will be able to save more time at the time of colleges and such. You know one thing the school people know about this. So it is not that unique of an idea.

Let's take it like this weird situation is here. Suppose if a mother has to ask about school fees from a father. Definitely father is going to take care of the kids very sincerely and with personal attention, because? He is a father, there is no question about his attention towards his children, and they all are one family, one unit. Same is true with the mother.

But the school or any educational institute is not a single unit. Although this is something they are also familiar with and they are trying to pretend the best to be one single unit. Which is not possible. Once we get to a school even for pre-primary school, the person we are going to meet for the first time, is not going to be the same person who will take care of our kid. In the reception front area, the very first unit, ask yourself are the people on reception area are going to spend their whole the time with their parents, they are trained enough to take care of the parents, NOT THE KIDS.

I started visiting couple of schools in neighbourhoods and around the area. I thought I was going to talk to the school, in whose hands my kid is going to be. I considered them one single unit, and this is a mistake. This is what I have found, I even heard so many common lines there too.

1. Look at the infrastructure of our schools,
2. Our school is following CBSE/MP Board/ICSE, or such system.
3. Our bus facilities.
4. Our teaching staff is this much qualified.
5. Our principal is having this much experience at school.
6. We have different section for kids.
7. The teaching methods are like this, so that kids could learn the best,
8. Look at the percentage of students in board exams.
9. We are topper in this, our school have received this award, that award.
10. Play area is matchless.

All so many such lines that could convince that this is the best school for my kid. But all of these lines are being told by a person who has his job at convincing you that how much you need this school. And they are going to do that anyhow. Because it's their job. They are representing school. And write in their resume that my admission closing ratio is 5 parents meeting out of 10, whenever they decide to switch their job for a better salary.

Let me ask you a simple question. What is the purpose of any of such representative sitting at the front desk of the school? I really wish the purpose could possibly be "The best education for the student's best and happiest life". But sadly this purpose is not something I could find anywhere.

This unit is called sales, and they are doing their best to get more sales into the school. If you will look towards it more closely there are so many things you will also find.

1. Advertisement in newspapers as the best school in the city has opened. Why we are best, and after this similar lines are written as if they are going to say on the front desk.
2. Similar advertisement in the radios.
3. In the Television.
4. Broachers.
5. Hoardings.
6. They even sponsor events too. Just to get than their name reminded to people.

7. Creative ideas for the attraction of parents, like a creative infrastructure to attract parents. To convince this is the best environment.
8. Sales people who are going to even talk door to door.
9. There are tons of methods these people are going to use.

Big money is being spent over these, and where will this money will come from? No doubt from students, and people call it a system. Again the same doubt appears I am also ready to pay for the best of my kid. But the question is same, is any of these activity or these tons of bucks has been spent for the better education? The answer is again a big NO.

So front desk, the very first unit, no wonder why it is the best construction of the school, because the parents are going to be there often.

"Let us remember: One book, one pen, one child, and one teacher can change the world."

- Malala Yousafzai

Years ago when my son was in 2nd grade, I visited one school of a big international brand. What happened there was, could help us in understanding it too. First at the entry they were having visitor's cards to be issued saying that nobody's entry is there without a card. At the front desk I could go through automatic card locked system gates. An entry guard did our entry and allowed to get there. My kid was not willing to get to the new school but he was with us that day. At the very entry there was an expensive kid's area with so many big toys. A maid came to us, she took our kid and sent him to a play area started involving him with those toys. The kid was happy. Now two beautiful ladies came to us, and asked us to fill a form of the details so that they could know about us. Some weird details like how much do we earn. How come did we heard about them, and such? After the form filled up. One of them took the form and second one took us to visit the whole school. She showed us lifts said that all lifts are being operated by cards every kid will have their own card and no kid's card is capable to take life somewhere else than his class and his play areas, cctv cameras are here, she make us visit the kids area, play area, class rooms, interactive things through which kids are going to learn, with all the classroom's books arranged of school syllabus only, with some story books, the canteen, where few teachers were taking their breakfast. They made us visit the school classrooms too, where couple of students were there. There coincidently I met one of my classmates who was working already there as a teacher. Everybody was smiling and the people the area was all seeming good. Than after they got me to the counselling people, and they asked me all the dates when are we going to take admission of kid, how did we find the school, and finally after an hour my kid was so happy. My wife so happy and got excited to take admission too.

Than my classmate called me later the same day, she said how's the life going on, and that was great seeing you after a very long time. Than later on she asked me

"So how did you find the school, did you like it",

I said

"Yes didi (Elder sister) I did like the school my wife is also liking the school and we are planning for my son's admission this year only."

She said

"Okay Rahul, what I am going to tell you keep this thing with you only. The school people tried to talk to me to approach you for the admission of your kid, and they want me to recommend this school to you, and offered me commission on the school fees too, but they don't know how our relations were, so being elder to you, don't admit your child in that school, but when they call you for follow up, which they will please do say that I recommended you and don't give them an exact date."

I asked with a big shock

"What happened Didi, is everything okay there?"

she said so many bad things about the school which only an internal person could have said, but the bottom line I still remember that she said "Everything which glitters is not gold, Rahul I am going to leave that school anyways in some time, they put too much work load as a teacher for me there." I asked

"Didi, you are supposed to teach junior class students what kind of pressure they can give you in teaching drawings"

She said

"Rahul, that's how normal people think, that I have to take care of only students, students are never a problem, who don't like to spend time with young kids, say for 8 to 10 years, but that's not the issue, issue is there management, politics, and above all, if I just have to teach students I would have given more than my 100%, but the thing is, I have to take care of notice board of each floor, and almost all of them, I need to decorate them, every festival every week, need to make props, decoration, not just that, annual function, any festival function I need to create all the props and have to take care of decoration, meetings are more than classes."

"Oh my god didi, rest other subject ones?"

I asked with shock. She said

"Every teacher has got similar situation here, few subject teachers work with me in overtime too when the work load increases".

I asked her

"Didi we were sincerely willing to get admission in the school, this is disappointing, as you are working in this schooling, can you please suggest any other school where should I be taking my kid to for admission?" she said

"Look brother, as you are close to me, I would have to say, I am teaching from like 13 years, and been at almost 6 schools and in touch with almost all the teachers around the school, every school has similar situation here, they all are in competition with each other",

Then she gave me couple of schools name can be counted on fingers, she didn't recommended me the best way, she said these schools are not worst, but focuses on education a little better.

> "School is a building which has four walls with tomorrow inside."
>
> \- Lon Watters

This was seriously soul breaking for me. But was all saying is, if we ask the same question again to ourselves, what could be the purpose of schools for doing all these? And the bigger question is, in this weird purpose of them each and every activity is leading to make parents happy, where the education of kid is being focused? All the efforts, money, and time is being consumed by them is not for the education of kids. And by any means, if the teachers are going to spend their time in these activities, how will they ever be able to focus and manage time even for the sake of education of kids.

> "Without Language thought is a vague uncharted nebula."
>
> \- Ferdinand de Saussure

Once I was taking a lecture and I met a student. He was something 22 year old and sincerely working very hard to clear a government exam called MPPSC, he was trying to study when I met him, all though he was there to understand and make group on English language, definitely he was looking to get command over English language for his exams preparation. When I saw his table he was having same book in two languages I thought I may be seeing wrong. I went to his table and I took a closer look. The two books were not just seeming as if they are same both the books were exactly the same year in publishing even the publisher was same. So I was having a kind of question

"Why do you have same book in two languages one language was Hindi and one language was English."

He said

"Good morning sir, actually the thing is I was initially in a government Hindi medium school my parents were not capable enough to send me in a private school initially, show in that government school I got to understand Hindi language and books very comfortably, when I was passing 7th standard my parents were more concerned about my career as the thought I am a bright student and I'll be able to solve there week economic condition too. Sort of their capacity they took and choose a private school which was not in their ability even to pay fees of it. But my father started taking couple of education loan on me my whole books and the medium of language changed suddenly to English language I was we get English and everybody was saying me to put more efforts on English language then Hindi as I was comfortable in Hindi I was knowing about it. So I started working hard on English, It took many years for me to read the book properly to understand it and I am still struggling to learn for that in the same way. Nobody in my circle speaks English everybody speaks Hindi around me so I am not able to practice my communication in English and that is why I am here with you."
I asked again

"Okay I get it son but the thing I am still wondering as you were comfortable in Hindi and you are here to learn English so why do you have the book of Hindi language?"

Now he was having a little smile on his face as if he made a mistake or something and he said

"Actually sir the thing is in English medium school after passing 10th class we had two choose one subject out of couple of subjects, in which physical education computer and Hindi is one of them, if we will choose Hindi then computer and physical education won't be there, and almost everybody choses either computer or the physical education ,computer because they believe computer is future of industry, and they will be able to make good career out of it, and the people who usually take physical education as part of education the main reason being is it is easy to increase percentage score through physical education, and almost nobody suggest or consider Hindi language as one of the useless subject to choose and almost nobody choses that, I am also one of those students, so it's been more than 6 years I have not written Hindi or I didn't get to study in Hindi, and the result is I am neither able to read everything in English as I was struggling for it even from the date I started my preprimary education and I am not able to get it, I was familiar with Hindi language initially but now the situation is as I left Hindi medium school my Hindi got weak, and as a result of English medium school from last 8 years I am not able to understand Hindi language books completely too. So now I can understand Hindi but I cannot understand Hindi books completely not knowing the Hindi language completely. And similar situation is with English as well. I know Nether Hindi nor English."

His last line about the languages is still in my head in neither know English nor Hindi.

"The Limit of my language mean the limit of my world."

- Ludwig Wittgenstein

The situation gets more complicated when he comes to a situation, when he is studying, and he gets to some words, which he neither gets in English nor in Hindi, he said.

"Sir, Sometimes, I try to google its similar meanings and if I don't find any, then
I have to drop that."

While reading books he was trying to read a paragraph or a line in English book then if there is something he didn't understand him go through the same line and same program in the book of Hindi. In the same book of Hindi he often didn't get couple of words at that time he uses Google to understand those words. I am not sure what kind of education he is already into if he is struggling for language. Language is going to be the medium to understand anything but if languages the barrier to understand things then there has to be something which is wrong.

In India we have got a kind of education system in which there are certain things which are responsible somehow for a kind of changes which even the person who made the education system was not knowing about. And this is one of the change I am talking about a consequence of selection in education system what it should include and what it should not.

Through all the weird ways in our vision somehow, the person who is going to be with students or going to teach, is somehow almost out of reach. And we won't be able to meet them, at least at the very first time.

A friend of mine was willing to open a school, whenever I talk to him he always talks about the profits of opening a school to me. I got chance to have a tea at his place, he was sitting in sofa with me. Tea came to hall with biscuits. His kids were watching You tube's some kids video, and me and my friend both were having tea in our hands, eyes on television, and kids, kids were enjoying the video. Suddenly an advertise came up, my friend asked his kids with a little louder voice

"Stop stop, don't skip this advertise, I want to see this",

There was a spontaneous excitement in him, his eyes were sparkling, and he was listening to that advertise so carefully, I still remember his face. Then I looked at the face of kids, almost at the age of 4 5, one girl and a body, both were also looking at their father, as if they are not at all understanding the excitement of father,

As if they were saying

"This boring weird people saying something rubbish and our father is behaving as if they are going to get whole world through it, this excitement and happiness is rarely seen even when he plays with us."

The advertise was of a branded school chain, which was showing the profits of opening a school through them, I still remember the key points they were mentioning, again the sales people who have made the video in a kind of direction to earn profit and make sale of school chain. The lines of the advertisement were like,

If you open this school,

You don't need much space,

You don't need much qualifications,

You don't need big staff,

They were decreasing every requirement required for the education. They even talked about

You just need this much amount to invest,

This much space, and

These little things to begin this partnership,

They will be managing everything and through that school chain once opened.

You will be able to earn lakhs of profit.

Than advertise got over. Just after advertise, my friend said

"Did you hear that?"

With full of excitement.

"this idea is all over brother, I really believe I should be opening a school, I will be able to be rich way earlier through this school, school is a necessity, I just have to provide facilities to kid and parents, I can get qualified teachers at very low cost, pre-primary teachers are even working at 3000, 4000, 6000 rupees (INR, Indian rupees) a month, very easy to find, and I will be rich"

I still wonder is opening a school should be money oriented?

Or is there anyone actually focusing over the true education of kids, future of world?

Is approach of my friend towards getting rich is something very unique?

Is the education is just a money making idea?

All the excitement, was it about making the life of a student, a kid?

Or it was all about getting rich?

Is making money through schools or education is his own idea?

Or some external source is trying and wanting him to think like this and make a school for their profit?

Is that external source's purpose if having any purpose of making a better education?

Aren't kids are in much better direction of enjoying life, and not willing to understand this weird ideas of not looking at what is more important?

Was this advertisement came up to him by chance?

Or were there a kind of strategy for this advertise to get to him? Trap should be a better word may be.

Is this whole making money idea is worth even to take the happiness of kids even for a second through advertise?

"Education is for improving the lives of others and for leaving your community and world better than you found it."

- Marian wright edelman

There are so many questions most of them are still bouncing in my head.

What has happened to the world?

Or is there anything wrong in my mentality if I am wanting kids to understand and get the true education?

He said

"I searched all over google too, that what is the process of opening a school? How can I open the school? Requirements to open a school."

No wonder how he found that advertise, or in better words I should be saying this advertise found him. I am not sure if I should be calling it fishing or I should be calling it true intentions of creating a better place for students to live in.

Well the purpose is quite clear behind this all, but I wonder who is managing these all? And why is he doing it?

Let's try to understand the perspective in a little different way, there is a line I remember of person who used to sale agro care products in Punjab. By agro care he used to sale things which benefits agriculture and farmers to save the crops of them. Basically pesticides were there mainly, it is a huge and long list of pesticides he had. I was talking to him, and he told me how his products are being distributed to whole of the state and whole of the country actually. He also told me how sales people approach him for buying more of the products, that sales people are doing so many awareness programs how the farmers should take care of their crops so they could make better crops insect free and healthy crop. He said the products will sell, they have made so many advertisements to increase the sale of these agro care products. You should fill your stocks of products as the rainy season is coming everybody will come to you to buy these.

This entire idea seem okay, until the shop person made his opinion.
He said

"Rahul brother, they all are trying to make us buy these so called agro care products, but they are not agro care products. It is written at the back of every product that IT IS A POISON! Keep away from children and read very carefully and has to be used under professional guidance. But the truth is brother, suppose the professional says to use 100ml per acre and rest water has to be used for these pesticides, people like me here around the shops says to use something 200ml for better security much better results, the person who buys it is not someone who is going to spread these to crops, he is mostly the person who is going to sale these too around the neighbourhoods and guides them to use more than 300ml for them, and later on when the time come and the person who is going to use the pesticides over the crops increases up to 500ml or something more than ½ of litre in it. And says that with this the crop will be safe from insects. Now brother what happens is the crop the food is no longer a food, it has become poison in itself",

And then he said something I don't think I will ever forget

"Now out of all the 87lakh species of the world, only 1 creature decides to eat that crop, and every other creature rejects that poison" Can you guess the name of that creature?

Yes you are right. It's us.

I remember one line I read, I want you to read so.

"You didn't come this far to ONLY COME THIS FAR."

\- Anonymous

Than later on he made conclusion of his own experiences and said

"These greedy idiots are not understanding one simple thing, they have these words only on their mouth, sale 2 gallons of pesticide and get a microwave free from company, sale 5 gallons get a refrigerator free too as a gift and bonus incentives, they all are just busy in earning money, not even a single idiot is ready to accept the fact that what they are overall creating is poison only, and this poison is being taken by the kids of our own, it is like killing our own kids, they overall creating poison to earn couple of pieces of papers, and using those papers they are buying the same poison and eat it"

That experience was hair rising for me too.

This same thing and same situation is very true for our education system too, the whole education system has now become a money oriented and business oriented system and the crop may seem beautiful but it is all vacant inside. Everybody I trying to push students to learn facts and figures, both the sales people who are trying to sale those so called agro care products, and the business person too, they may have taken formal education, but are they actually educated? If they are educated then why they overall killing themselves. Not just them we all are overall supporting that agro care system as well as this so called education system.

If we talk about a solution oriented approach here, than the answer is simple, if it is again a possibility, I may have to ask you this. Is education is business? The definition of education will always be a mystery if we won't be able to clear this in our mind. Business is made for money, and for what purpose education is made for?

"The true purpose of education is to make minds, not careers."

- William Deresiewicz

What if the purpose of education is wrong?

"Education without values, as useful as it is, seems rather to make man a cleverer devil."

- C.S. Lewis

There is a line very famous on social media too, that we should be loving people and using things, but in actual, people are loving things and using people. Do you know the word people here have a vast identity? The people here mean everyone as human beings around us, including us. We all have very good intentions for our kids, and our loved ones for them to get a good education, but after spending years for them, lots of work, lots of money, and course all the struggle behind the intentions of having them good education. What happens is the kid starts behaving as an intelligent person, as what we believe, but the truth is we are overall using the word intelligence instead of clever devil, why am I saying this?

Everybody in the world is making the world, and the whole world falls into this category. This is almost true with almost every human in the world with a special education system. Let me take you through a little study.

In the health sector, India is among the top 30 corrupt countries in the world. What is the corruption here? During the time of COVID-19, the black market of human organs was something not very rare. When you visit the hospital still now too, they are going to ask the family first "What do you do?", so that they can know, how much money we can take from him. There is one more question "Do you have health insurance or a medical claim?" Killing a girl child during pregnancy is like killing a kid who can't speak, a very famous bad deed here. Doctors are considered to be saviours, they were considered gods in ancient times, and the person who saves a life is the one who gives life. You tell me, if a person is taking their life, what should we call him? I am not going to call him educated at least, but yes for the devil. A doctor is also considered one of the most educated people in the world. These doctors are not considering life as life. Not just doctors, it is just an example, for both private and government sectors.

There is a line as an act of goodness creates an endless ripple, it is true in the opposite sense too, and an act of badness also creates an endless ripple. In 2005 almost 62% of the people faced first-hand experience with the issue of bribery in India. It hasn't changed much till now. It's not like it is the situation of India only, it is the situation of almost the whole of the world. Education, police, land property, almost everything is there in this 62%. And they all are considered to be educated, because to have a job anywhere, you need to be educated, and these all are being done after so-called education.

Almost 85% of people in the job sector hate their job, hating a job, means hating the 7 9 hours of their day, which they continue to do for their whole life. Almost everyone in the sales have convinced themselves that they are not lying, but they are. There is a line for sales Salespeople lie to promote their agenda, not yours. They don't believe they lie because they don't give you false information. They don't blatantly tell you a lie. They don't tell you something that is straight up not true and so because they don't directly lie; they've convinced themselves they aren't lying. With this aspect, they don't even care what their lives are going to affect, what will you call them? Educated people? Or the person who is doing wrong, thinking as if it is a compulsion for them to make their survival?

Not just that, People appreciate and support these bad deeds by so many such lines, as

1. There is a need for competition.
2. We have to survive, that's why have to do this.

3. To be successful in this industry you have to do this.
4. If he doesn't do that, he will lose his job.
5. He has to do this because of family.
6. What option does he have?

And with all these doings and compulsions, can a person who knows he is not doing good deeds, can make a better society?

Let me ask you this.

1. Is this what we are looking for in our society?
2. Is this why we spend our lives for our kids or our family?
3. Is this going to be worth, even for our generations for themselves too?

Our children are going to spend their whole life hating their work, almost more than half of their life they are going to spend. Let's take this to a little more solution-oriented perspective and a better direction from here.

"Early childhood education is the key to the betterment of society."

- Maria Montessori

People believe that education is going to make society a better place to live, whatever we discussed about the current scenarios of society is better or not? I wish I could say this, but I want you to think about it first, we did everything to make society a better place to live. So is society better now? Or it was better? Let me ask you this,

When a kid plays with his friends he is so much happy, when he draws any drawing he is 100% present there, When a kid is somewhere, he is 100% there, with no regrets, a sadness can stay for a couple of moments only, they are always loved almost by all of us. And they are almost always confused, why should I take education?

They don't know the meaning of a better person, an employee, or a job either, but they are content, when they are with their family, they have got plenty of time, and always content.

I have asked so many people in my life, they are educated but have no such qualities in them, when they play with friends, they have their minds still stuck on family or professional issues, it's so hard to find a person who is content, and almost nobody draws now.

So if a kid is confused about education, why should he study? I asked myself too, do I want my kid to be educated and not as happy as he already is? Do you want this life how people are educated and not at all content?

The problem is way vaster than it seems here, the kind of confusion he has got is indeed right! Of course, the question is not like 2+2 is 4. It doesn't work like this, right? There has to be a proper answer, and the weird truth is there is no proper answer. It is like measuring an art piece that doesn't have any measurement scale.

I am not judging here, because if I had given him another better answer to the question of why should we study, that would have been an answer to my perception there is no such definition of right or wrong here, but this is right for sure. We are the generation who is witnessing the whole world upgrading itself, and so is education, for example I phone 14 to iPhone 15, android version 1.0 to 2.0, and we do that to make it better, right?

Education is also being taken from the same perspective, authorities are changing syllabuses like they are introducing new software, and new technologies to education, I got a chance to even read a book for the 6th class that had Adobe animate in their school syllabus. What I am trying to say is version 2.0 should be better than version 1.0 too, right?

We are sending our kids to school to become their upgraded version, something similar or better than us, but the question here is do we live our life happier than a kid? Come on, version 2.0 should be better than 1.0 right? Our upgraded version is happier or the previous version was happier? Our previous version was healthier or our upgraded version is healthier? If it is not better than we are not upgrading, and my words could be a little harsh here, if we are not upgrading, we are downgrading?

None of us would want our kid to be a downgraded version of us or themselves, so If the education will be good enough, it surely going to make stronger youth, stronger people, and so the nation will become strong too. By strong I didn't mean only the physical strength.

So let's talk about a solution oriented approach here, what I am trying to say is, almost 1/3 of every school's budget is used for sales. What do they actually do with this budget? Every advertisement platform asks for money, a lot of money. And once the people at the top of the education system or institutions are focused on money, they don't often think about the true development of the kid. But what if the commercialization of school is not available?

There are plenty of countries where it is not allowed to open a school, by any private organization. In Norway all the schools are always free to attend, and even for international students. No private organization means no greed. No greed means no business involved with education. And no business mean only government officials are taking care of it not just that, the education is free, universal and same for all. No comparison in big school or small school, no comparison in rich or poor, no comparison in educational guidelines, no comparison means no jealousy, no disappointment, and no disappointment in students or parents about the schools and institutions means a happier, cleaner, and student's oriented education system. Do you know 24 countries have less than 2% of privatization in education? And 73 countries are having less than 10% of privatization in education. And in comparison with students too, their education is doing way better than the other countries. It's a fact available on google too. Sales should not be a part of education, I am strongly against of it. And I really believe this time of people this cost of sales should be utilized for the betterment of students. Better students, means better humans, means better society, means better countries, means better world. Shouldn't this be the purpose of education? Or the purpose of schools or institutions is to make and focus on money?

Now definitely I am not judge here, all I am trying to make a better education for all of us.

So let's get to a solution oriented exercise here. From your perspective too. I want you to continue the task we did previously about the purpose of education.

Now with the purpose of education, what was the reason you chose the institute or school? Please try to write down every education like the previous one you mentioned, or after the same place you write that down.

Now about the activity, whatever the institute, school where you have taken education or somewhere any of your loved one has taken admission, I want you to write down, did you meet only the front desk people? Or did you meet the teachers too? Try to note down the same in front of it.

Next time you visit any school, I don't want you to be a pain for them, but I want you to make sure, that our kid gets what he deserves, if you are in an institute than you deserve a lot in your life, please go for that. Remember

"Before starting anything, the good purpose should be crystal clear in our mind."

- Rahul Bajad

Please highlight good purpose.

Necessity 4

Attitude

"Attitude is a little thing that makes a big difference."

\- Winston Churchill

Once I was going to have some restaurant with my kid, in front of that there was a public water system, where everyone can fill up there water requirements for free. There were so many taps, but only one tap was working, so there was a big line of some people who were waiting for their turn to fill their buckets. Out of curiosity my son asked

"Papa (Father), why is it so, that there is a big line of people on one tap of water only, why no one is standing at the other taps. The tap they all are waiting for is quite dirty, the other ones seems colourful, quite clean, and better."

I said with a smile,

"It's not about how the taps looks, or seem to be son, It's what they have got inside, it's what they deliver to people, it's what how much they can serve is what matters son!"

Isn't it true for us as well? Although later I thought, the line has got a way wider meaning, may be helpful to understand the value of attitude.

The monitor of the class is usually not the student with highest marks, the person who gets promotion is not always the person who is most constructive, he is usually not the person who works hardest for the company. Our classmates who were topper once in our class are not necessarily the one who are more successful in life, neither the back benchers are the people who are very unsuccessful in life, what moves us ahead, what gives us the actual power is something inside of us. It is actually the attitude of the person.

I was studying a lecture of a doctor once over depression and issues with the people's life, I still remember one line of the professor.

"Problem is not the actual problem of life, it's how we react to it."

A similar line I have heard is I remember for us is.

"Life is 10% of what happens to you, and 90% how you react to it."

- Charles R. Swindoll

This is something even we should all expect from education too. The perspective of seeing something is going to decide the attitude of one. And how we see things is what matters the most. Attitude is overall a person's way of thinking about something or someone. Or one may say it's about evaluating someone or something. We can also say that it is also a kind of tendency to respond positively or negatively to a person, it's not necessarily a person, it could be an idea, it possibly can be an object, someone's thought on something, but most importantly how we see a situation is something I am mostly concerned over.

The reason being, we tend to plan something always, but it's not like whatever we are going to plan is going to be reality, consider an example of mountain climbing. We always tend to get at a higher position in our life, just like getting to the peak of a mountain.

When we decide to get to a mountain, we first make a target, then we make a plan to get to it, and we start following that plan, from the beginning to the end, but is that plan is going to be exactly successful, the exact path he chooses changes with time, the plan he makes has to be changed as he takes the milestones, if he won't change the plan, he may fall from the mountain, just like the people fall from the path of their life goals and success. He has to change the plan he has to change the path a little or more, as per the situation. And this is where the ability to see things in the best possible way is the attitude here.

Overall if you really want to get peak of the mountain or you want to get to a goal of yours. Your attitude is something that is going to decide everything.

"Attitude is everything, so pick a good one."

\- Wayne Dyer

Once I went for a lecture in a reputed school in a little far area here, as an artist, my lecture was going to be for the art. But before the lecture, I get to meet with the principal of that school.

"May I come in sir?"

I said.

"Come in, Come in, and take a seat son."

He said. I have to say that was energising, And just after that.

"So Rahul, Have you got experience in teaching the senior students."

I said,

"Yes sir, I have been teaching school students, college students, even those students too who are pursuing masters, from years actually."

He wasn't looking that so much impressed. And as I believe work should speak louder than words. So I said.

"Sir the best I can say here is, give me a chance to prove myself, if I couldn't you won't be seeing me again."

Now he smiled, and said.

"You see Rahul, I can see your portfolio and experience, definitely you can teach students, as you have been taking lectures from years, and I can see the list of colleges and school where you have taken lectures, But."

Now even I was curious, then what could he possibly doubting at. He continued.

"But the thing is Rahul, You have been teaching city students, and this school is a little out of city, although a reputed school it is, so we get so many city students as well as village students too, as we have got so many villages around this area. So they might find it difficult to understand you. Or you may find it difficult to teach them. Rich village, 0 etiquettes students, especially I mean"

Now I smiled, and said.

"Sir let the work talk, I can talk about the content of the lecture, but when I see student, I may find, what is requirement of student."

I sincerely believe, everyone is unique, and every student may need a little different treatment, He smiled and he was in big confidence and said.

"I may not be able to explain you, Now Let me talk a little straight here, you may have taught students, but these 12th class students are not students, they are Devils. All the time I get complains from them, they all almost hate each other, all the time they fight with each other's like animals."

I was in shock, a big one. But as he was a principal, I took his words and said.

"Possibly sir, let's take the class, then we will talk about it."

A teacher took me to the class, while walking, I asked the same question to that teacher.

"How are the students of the class sir?"

"Very dangerous sir, one of the student once threw a chalk too at me. They are almost like a devil. Behaves like uneducated rich kids, who respects no one."

I was surprised to know a little, and I was thinking the same thing now, possibly they may have got this mischievous attitude or something. While I was walking, I saw a sports teacher, shouting really bad at a student there, just because of wrong throw in the basket.

And reached the class in a while. There I actually noted, that only few students stood up and few didn't, barely 40% students wished good morning, and rest were not that much interested. And as it was a demo lecture. So I began.

"Very Good morning friends!"

Now in response I got couple more of wishes, more than 40% as it was initially. Then I made an offer directly.

"So friends, I have got a deal for you, Weather you like it or not, I am going to be here for 40 45 minutes, either you or I can make this time happy and memorable. Or you want me to take a boring lecture like few of our friends yawning at back. You call."

Now the percentage of students who were taking interest increased. Now I got to another step, I introduced myself, and asked for their introduction but in a little different way.

"So friends, possibly today is my first or last day here, totally depends on you, if you won't like me, I won't be coming back, but if this 40 minutes will be happy, and if you all will say, I will be back for next lecture too. So I have got a game to play then we will talk about education if you will say."

Now with the word game few more students got interested. I continued. When most of them said yes.

"Loud and clear friends."

They all shouted very loud, as they were mischievous, I gave them a simple task and offered one chocolate whom so ever will do that best.

"So friends, i have given my introduction here, and the game is your introduction, I want you to give yours, but if you all will speak, I may not be able to hear all of them, so I want you to take out your notebook. And on the page write down your name, at the top of it."

After 2 minutes,

"I asked them, now what you have to do is, I want you to give your paper to your friend and ask him to write one good line of introduction about you, on that paper, and pass the same paper to other friend, and I want you all to write one good line of the person whose paper comes to you. A good introduction from your friend's perspective. Whosoever will have answer of my question in the introduction page, is going to get the chocolate. Remember that you have to write one good line what you believe as the quality of that friend of yours. Now begin!"

Initially the students who were not taking interest, got interested too, come on, everybody wants to hear something good about what other think of them, in 15 minutes all the papers were done. I called all the papers on table, few were still writing, but I got them all in a while, I asked one of the student to come to me and distribute that paper to the student's whose name is on the top. Without saying anything they were so much curious to read that. But I still said.

"So you have got 5 minutes to read these all first, than we will decide whose introduction is the best one."

After 5 minutes, I want you to believe, few of the students had wet eyes, most I saw pin drop silence in class, what was something even the school didn't hear from that class. Everyone was so much curious. Everyone was willing to know what others think about them, what their friends think about them. Now I asked.

"Okay times up, it's time to announce the winner, are you all ready?"

"YES!" they all were cheered up.

I said, okay then, I took one chocolate out of my pocket, Put that on the desk in front of everyone and said.

"So before announcing the winner, I want you all to decide, whom so ever believes, that whatever 10 good lines written on the paper are all wrong about himself, and he or she believes that this isn't me, can come and grab the chocolate."

At this stage the whole class was looking at me, and somehow they all were happy, and were willing to hear more from me, and no one was wanting to take the chocolate.

"So I asked, I am happy for you all, now I want you to do one final favour for me? Can you do that?"

Everybody was listening to me at that time, I just asked them

"You all have to write one good line about the principal sir, who is outside right now. Think a little more, whatever good you may have noticed about him, anytime of the year or your school journey, and write that in one line."

You won't believe just because of this activity, even after a year, the kids were having that paper safe, few of them have laminated that paper, but that wasn't the achievement, the students suddenly became friendly with each other, the complains of basic quarrels and fights their mischievous ness suddenly dropped to almost 0.

I still remember that day, when the class got over. Couple of the students came to me when I left the class and were saying like,

"Sir we are sorry we may have misbehaved with you initially"

One student followed me till the moment I got alone a little, and when he got chance he stopped me there, according to class he was one of the most mischievous student, and said

"Excuse me sir, First I am so sorry, I didn't take you as a good teacher initially, but actually everyone as teacher and principal sir thinks we are villagers, and we won't get good antiquates or good behaviours like educated city people, they all usually talks good at our faces, but it feels like they all considers us Devils, as if we are animals, so we all started to behave as if we are not good too. But this paper you gave me, I used to think that everyone thinks bad about me, as few of us are from village, but they think really good about me, and I felt really really bad for my bad deeds. I am so sorry sir, and thank you so much for this paper too, we won't ever misbehave with any student or any teacher from now."

His words were not just touching, the attitude was something which was creating the biggest problem here too from my perspective. As I always say I am not judge for sure. But seeing a devil in the student, is something that will make him a devil.

Now let's get to a solution oriented approach here, how we can solve this and make our loved once the most powerful attitude holders. There is one powerful solution I have got.

Think of a situation like this, all the kids at their initial stages know nothing about almost everything, we start teaching them everything, mother father teacher, everyone starts explaining everything to them, almost about everything, as they know nothing initially, whatever we try to explain them or tell them, that is right. They start to take every word of ours as truth. When we say that at evening guests would come, and when they see that guests have come, the starts believing that our mother knows everything. They usually couldn't connect that they might have received a call from guests.

When parents or teachers say, today is going to be hot, they usually don't connect that could be from newspaper or weather from google, they believe, parents are always right. When parents or teachers says today it will rain, they may say by seeing clouds too, but kids start believe wow, my parents always say the truth.

Now if a person is in some office work tension, and he scold his son, if son I wanting to play with him. And somehow as kids at their initial learning phases, they may spoil or suppose write on some office paper something, Even if the father is angry and says

"You are an idiot!"

They take it seriously, if a teacher says,

"You are dumb."

They take it as truth, and accepts inside of them. If a kid may somehow disturbs in mother's domestic work, you may have heard,

"You are a devil and you always bothers me a lot."

This becomes his identity. He takes the word inside. Or if a boy is crying.

"You cry like a girl."

It could be words for us. But it is truth for them, I have seen many parents' abuses their children, and they keep on doing that till their retirement comes, because that abuse initially, becomes their reality later on.

So a solution oriented thought is really really really simple, always say what you want them to be, like

My son is intelligent,

My daughter is obedient,

My student listens to me always.

My friend is loving.

I can understand, that sometime we may get into some situations, where emotions get out through mouth in not that good way, that time, whenever you are saying anything negative, always use "BUT". As an example.

Kid you are dumb, but you are becoming good, and one day you will be great.

You disturbs me often, but you are becoming understanding day by day, and understanding enough that the good girl don't disturbs the work, and

Let teacher take his class or

Let father do his work.

Or let mother do the dishes.

I promise you the results will be amazing.

Bottom line,

"Never leave the sentence incomplete, if it is negative, always end the sentence in positive."

If we will change the attitude of saying, looking at them, looking at things, so will become of theirs too. And this is how their character and attitude, and life will be as amazing as possible.

Let's end this chapter on a good note too. I remember a story in one of the holy book, the story of Krishna (Considered as god), the story is like, and Once Krishna gets to Hastinapur. Hastinapur is basically a place where the whole Mahabharat (It's the name of the event happened in the life of Krishna, as well as it is the name of the holy book too) happened. So Krishna reached hastinapur, and he met both Yudhishthir, and Duryodhan.

As per the story, Duryodhan is villain in the story and a bad person. Yudhishtir is the hero in the story, never lies, and a good person. So Krishna met both Yudhisthir and Duryodhan. It was about the comparison between the attitudes of both. He asked both of them one by one. He asked duryodhan than go and find a good person in whole hastinapur. Similarly he asked Yudhishthir that go and find a bad person in whole hastinapur.

After a while duryodhan came back to Krishna and says, everyone is bad in hastinapur

“I couldn’t find anyone who is good in here.”

Surprisingly Yudhishthir came back after a while too, Krishna asked the same questions, and so did you find any bad person. While Duryodhan was pretty sure as everyone is bad in hastinapur, but in a contrasting way, Yudhishthir said,

“I couldn’t find anyone, who doesn’t have goodness in themselves.”

If the attitude is right, you are like a light in that case, you will see light in everyone and everything. Not just that you will spread the light around yourself too. All a student in actual need is a powerful and good attitude. And if a person is having a good attitude, he can create wonders. But it is something which can be given to anyone, from the person who has a good one.

Take the example of newspapers, the ones who see the world through news, are keeping the perspective from the news itself. You will often hear from them, the world isn't good enough, you know that this bad has happened to the neighbour of that person. Usual trust issues. It's not like that no one has light inside.

"Where there is a wish there's a hope."

- Rahul Bajad

Necessity 5

Honesty

"May we think of freedom, not as the right to do as we please but as the opportunity to do what is right"

-Peter Marshall

What I truly believe for a teacher to do best and give the best of education for students. He has to first think best for them. A bird in a cage can think of anything but freedom. Suppose if a person can see bad, but because it is not allowed for them to do something they starts ignoring it and a famous line pops up.

"Let's mind our own business".

It could possibly through compulsion, through will, through capabilities, or may be the person could be like this. But above it there has to be freedom at handling their own work at the minimum, right? If they will be pressurized to do something else than their job at priority. Then the job is no longer a priority.

Let's talk it through another way, I shortlisted couple of schools for my kid at his pre-primary education, and I started visiting many schools in a row, I am a self-employed person and like usual my kid is my first priority. So selecting the best place for him was my priority just like everyone. I will be honest, in this process I met so many greedy people, the ones which we just talked about, and everybody is just looking for admission for the sake of money. All they were looking for is just one more admission, as I mentioned, we are going to meet sales people, the front desk, than the administration and their rules bounded people.

But I wasn't that unlucky. At the 3rd day of my investigation, I should be saying, I get to meet a powerful personality, I am not talking about school, but somehow I get to meet the actual person who was going to teach and be with my kid somehow, off course mistakenly but that happened. I still remember her name was Diya mam, she was class teacher of my kid. I was in the counselling section of my kid education that was a kind of interview round questions and answers were there, the same process got to visit the school in which I wasn't so much interested in, in the middle of it, I got the visit the going to be class of my son. Diya mam, who was interacting with kids of similar age of his. I didn't get chance to talk to her, but somehow she had to get something and accidently she saw my son, she wasn't knowing I was looking at her that time, my son was playing a little my wife was with the counsellor. His teacher took my kid in her arms, she was very comfortable and my kid got comfortable with her too in the very first meeting, and that was odd. And guess what, my kid was not wearing diaper that time and he peed, I was looking at the face of that teacher very closely there was not even a single little bad or weird expression on her face all the time, as if nothing happened just like a mother could do. You know what I am glad he peed that day, I am glad he didn't wore a diaper that day. That lady made him made him all ready again, his cloths, made the kid comfortable again and my kid started playing again. No communication happened with us that day. But his class teacher Diya mam got on my Radar that day. Trust me I still remember the face expression of Diya mam, and my son's too.

> "Teaching is love in its purest form."
>
> \- T J Herrmann

Before we go a little more deep towards, I have got one simple question, can you say what could possibly be her intentions towards my kid, towards his education. They are crystal clear. I got chance to meet Diya mam so many time after that and those intentions of her, and the vibrations I got through her were as pure as water.

The thing is, nothing else mattered to me that day, neither the syllabus of school, nor the education system they may have, and this is what I want to convey. Can any teacher ever have bad intentions about any student? The answer is a big NO! And if intentions are pure and if the overall result is not satisfactory still, then the process must have something to take care of.

There is one more important thing to be considered here, I got chance to meet the person who was going to be with my son as student. And this is what clears the path. Getting a chance to meet the teacher instead of administration or the sales front desk people. Take my words as it is a blessing. And is the best way to get what we actually are looking for. Intentions are often clear, no teacher in the world will ever want wrong for their student. So let's find out the issue. And it's necessary.

"It's a teacher that makes the difference, not the classroom."

- Michael Morpurgo

You may also have seen so many teachers faking in front of students that they are best and doing the best they can, but as I have learned too this fakeness is always visible. They say

"If the smile is not honest, then it's irritating."

- Anonymous

I have seen so many teachers faking their intentions in front of students. But if the students are not around, true colours often appear visibly. So once I get a chance to meet an English language trainer at a reputed institute. And was somehow in the middle of a discussion about the topic of how to grow. They were discussing how we grow and how can we make things around us better. As there were no students around us at that time, in that discussion. One faculty named Virendra sir, said a powerful line that I still remember, he said

"There is only one way we can grow, and that is we have to provide Quality Education."

This single line clearly shows that his intentions towards education and students are vital, and he is sincerely wanting the students to understand, learn and be powerful in his subject. I really love this mind-set.

If we consider the Pareto principle also known as 80-20 rule, that there are only 20 out of 100 teachers are there who are doing 80% of the work. So finding such teachers is already not a piece of cake. Above it, there is another issue that you won't get to meet the teachers at the very beginning ever. They are considered to be the backstage artists. If we go to any school or any institution we are going to meet the front desk which has got people trained enough to get admission. They are trained to get admission not to think about the kid whether we have what it requires to fulfil the kid's educational needs or not. They are focused on the admission of them.

And the weird truth is the management is never going to listen to the backstage artists as teachers, who are going to be with the students all the time. So the happening is no matter how good a teacher has got intention to do something good for students the best they have in their hand is whatever they are getting as admission with whatever syllabus and methods the admission and administrative staff or process has decided they have to follow it. The result becomes a mess in itself, one singular unit of education is no longer a single unit now. And this creates a kind of environment where the intention of making a kid's future brighter becomes a wish only.

"The direction in which education starts a man will determine his future life."

- Plato

There was a student in the 10th class I had once, was coming to me, but he hardly studied, and he never even tried to focus on studying however I tried. I always used to wonder what I should be doing for him. Even when exams were close, all his classmates used to study, but he didn't. I thought his result would be a blunder. Whenever I asked him to study, he always had this cute smile, winked at me, and said

"Sir you worry too much, Chillax! I have got a magic wand"

This chillax was neither 'chill' nor 'relax', and this mysterious magic wand was out of my thought process.

Later on, sweets were offered by him with the same cute smile, and he said sir

"Here is the result sir, you will be proud of me",

I saw the results and it was shocking that 67% were made. I congratulated him, and asked with curiosity

"This is a good result for you son, how come you made this?"

And he said the same lines

"Sir you worry too much, Chillax! I have got a magic wand."

I laughed a little and he went back to his home.

Do you know what his magic wand was? He had some unreasonable and non-trustable resources who somehow leaked the paper and he got them a night before the exam.

My question is, is it a magic wand? The answer is, it surely is not. If we try to find, we can find and point out the responsible problem here, the problem in the education system, that the paper got leaked, weirder the kid was already knowing about the paper going to be leaked. Corruption is a big issue, very hard to find the responsible one who did this bad of a deed, there is a big chain of authorities who forward those papers from central to the schools. But if we will talk about it I have to write another book on it. Let's try to see from a different perspective here.

Let me put it like this the problem here is this sentence "I have got a magic wand", In actual it is a poison, we are trying to find the solution from the top, and this way we will never get to solve this, Let me ask you this, Can a plant be greener if we start giving water to leaves? The answer is no! if you don't like the fruit, problem is with the root. Or as Harv sir said.

"If you want to change your fruit, you have to change your roots."

- T. Harv Eker

And the root is, the mind-set of the kid, let's see his perspective now, he used to play often, and he likes to play, why? Because that is interesting, the study is not. He was relaxed coz somebody in his circle was saying don't worry I will give you the exam papers. He made the choice not to study coz at a point he came to think that studying was not important enough, there was no need to leave fun for studying, it's a pity, it's small, it's not useful, it's boring. The biggest question of this mind-set is if education is what makes people successful, then why the richest people or successful people in the locality, or in their family, or in their circle, or even in social media are not that educated? What my teacher has done with this education, is riding a middle-class bike, and every student in my class is making fun of him, nobody respects the teacher in the class of a teacher who is educating us, so why should I study?

And this is where it is legging, imagine it like this, I am an Indian, and if I am going to any other country I will be representing India, right? If I am an engineer and I am going in between the doctors then I will be representing engineering, right? In the same exact way, the teachers and the surroundings are not just representing themselves, they are representing EDUCATION too.

If the education is being represented around him, like a teacher is being a piece of fun in front of whole class, it's not the teacher, it's the education who is being a piece of fun for the student. If a family member appreciates somebody who is not representing education in a good way, the mind-set of the student, mind-set of a kid suddenly changes and starts to consider that education is way less of a priority.

"Honesty is the fastest way to prevent a mistake from turning into a failure."

\- James Altucher

I remember an incident of a priest, or you may say indian pandit, who has got knowledge of god, almighty, all the holy books, he was talking about the stories of holy books in public, suddenly while everyone was trying to ask questions. A person raised his hand, the priest asked him,

"Yes please, say your heart."

He said

"Sir, I was having a question about good and bad deed, can I ask?"

Priest said

"Yes, please"

And he said

"Is it true, that if I will do bad things then I will be going to hell after death?"

Priest said

"Yes, you are right here, if you will do badly, after death the holy books of ours suggests that the person will go to hell."

Then he asked a counter question.

"If I am not doing badly, but if I am helping bad people then?"

The priest got curious here and said

"Then also, helping evil is evil, you may have to serve in hell. But why do you want to help bad people."

He said,

"Sir my profession is to help bad people. I am an advocate."

Priest said

"An advocate is somebody who advices, how could this profession be helping bad people."

He said,

"Sir, I have to get the bad people out of the jail, and then they again commit crime."

Priest said

"Why do you have to take the case of bad people, take the case of good people."

He said.

"Sir, there is almost no case in court of good people we can fight? Almost everyone who is coming to court are bad people."

Then the priest said

"Bad thing will be done on something or somebody less bad, or good, right? Why don't you fight against the bad people in that case?"

He said

"Sir, we can't fight cases from the side of victims or accused, government appoints a government advocate to fight for them. We can only fight from the person mostly who is a criminal or who has got allegation of crime."

Now the priest said out of more curiosity.

"Then why do you help them? try to find cases from good people there has to some."

He said.

"Sir, if I will wait for the cases of only and only good people, I may have to leave the profession because I may not be able to even earn my bread and butter. The good people usually don't have money, they won't be able to pay advocate's fees, and those who can pay the fees are usually not good people. So even to earn out bread and butter. We have to fight for the bad people as criminals. I used to do this with full energy and excitement when I was young, I am now 65 years old, and now I am worried about my deeds, how much time do I have to serve in hell, if I did badly"

"The power of choosing good and evil is within the reach of all."

- Origen

Suppose a doctor, a policeman, a judge, or an advocate is rich and famous, no offense to the profession, even if he is doing some bad things in his profession, saving bad people even after knowing that the person is doing bad. If a family member is now endorsing advocacy and saying my son, my daughter get educated so that you could be like him, he is going to be a really bad of person. And a bad person produces bad things. And this is how a society is being made. This is why we are not making a good society, this is how we are making a bad place to live for future generations too.

The student who has learned I should be educated enough to be like that successful and rich advocate. There will be one day, he will be successful and rich like that advocate parents, family, and circle was appreciating, but from my perspective, he will not be educated, possibly rich and famous, but not educated. Ask yourself does education mean being rich? Or being famous? Or it is in the mind of students that we have to get an education to be rich? Or to be successful?

"Success isn't about how much money you make, it's about the difference you make in people's lives."

\- Michelle Obama

Once I got a chance to meet a counselor. She was working in a private institute. And I came to know so many good things through her. The institute was for preparing the exams of NIFT, NID, and such designing careers. I was able to see the career there was so many good reviews of a students who got selected in the exam and topped in their career. They were charging very less fees and with that less fees they were providing so many facilities for the students as if it was a kind of social work.

I appreciated the counsellor and I said

"You are doing a wonderful work in the field of career guidance and helping the students who are actually willing to do something good in their career."

When I appreciated her she was in a cafeteria with a friend of mine and her in common. When I appreciated her she didn't thank me for that and she was looking at our friends face for a while and give me a smile. She was looking very educated and experienced I asked her out of curiosity that why you didn’t thank me at the minimum. She said

"Dear Rahul I really love the way you see things around you, but I myself do not like my job very much"

This was totally an unexpected answer for me she seemed happy with us having fun cracking jokes and she was saying she was not happy with confusion I asked

"Why is it so? You should be proud on yourself that you are doing a good deed and I believe on a good salary as well what is there not to like your job."

She smiled again and said

"Look around you Rahul, if you have seen my job as well this is a corporate place, it is the corporate building, everybody here is doing business, and somehow I am also doing a kind of business only."

I was having a kind of weird expression on my face now

"What are you talking about?"

I said. Now she answered me with the powerful line of her

"How many people have you ever seen doing a social work at a corporate place? Imagine it like this there are something around 30 students per batch, six faculties are here, rent of this place is very high which is also here, the institute we are operating is of a brand which we have to pay royalty as well, there is our salary as well, and the fees structure how we are taking from the kids is something not that much good enough to maintain all these"

I was not that surprised and said

"Yes I can see that, that is why I said it is almost a kind of social work and appreciate you for that"

Then she again smiled and said

"It is not the actual picture think like this there are something 4000 or 5000 seats are available for NIFT, and around 40000 50000 students are going to apply for that. As this course is something where are rich class usually apply as the course fee is so high. But almost 90% students are not going to be selected, there are something 16 centers available for NIFT all over the country, the top 100 people are going to get the desired place for them, and they are going to choose the best center of all the 16."

After hearing this with excitement

"I was not knowing about these numbers overall these 100 people beat the competition out of 40000 and you guys help them for that I have seen so many pictures in the newspaper as well of the toppers from your institute, it is a good thing"

Then she said

"Yes exactly, this is how they all want you to think like this."

Now with shock I said

"WHAT!"

She continued

"This 40000 and 50000 people are going to take admission in coaching classes for the preparation of exam in coaching institutes like us, now if any of these are going to top in exam say if there in top 100 we are going to take their pictures and put them on the wall as an achievement bigger the rank bigger the position of picture only 10% of the people are not going to use a coaching class direction for the admission, now as only 4000 or 5000 seats are available 80% of the people are not going to get a place and above 300 or 400 ranks a students are not going to get a desired center out of 16 so you can say the people who are going to choose other let us drop again to get into top 100 rank next year, or they have to take a private college for the education, now as we were giving guidance to students for the preparation of entrance exams we build trust in a students and they and their people as parents trust us for the guidance as we were not charging big education fees for guidance in our classes, now we recommended them names of private colleges and say that these colleges are better and way good for our kid, parents believes us and takes the student their child to these private colleges"

I was nudging my head and still confused

"This still seems a kind of help what are the issues you are talking about?"

Then with the bad expression she said

"The private colleges charge a big fees from the students Rahul, and we institutes are getting big commission out of these fees in lakhs, and this is actual the source of income for us, the 80% students who are going to fail are someone which are our concern which are going to give us way more of a profit then they are providing"

Now I felt bad, she continued

"If these collages are good enough for their career they could have been at the first place but they are not good colleges over all most of the students career is going to spoil they are going to pay so big amount of money and will not be able to make career out of our guidance, the 20% students who are going to top score good numbers in the exams if they belong to our institute we are going to utilize them for advertisement we are there permission put their pictures on our wall, and the weird thing is the student who scored very good marks are now going to endorse us if they are from our institute, definitely a hardworking gem is something can be found anywhere, so sometimes this also happen that the 10% who are not taking any coaching classes they is core better than the students who are into coaching classes like ours, now coaching classes like us pays a lot of money to those a students who didn't took any of the coaching class, and just like most of the celebrity who are promoting products which they do not use, we use them for advertisement to increase the sales and overall get more of the admissions"

Now I was disappointed

"But this is something completely wrong where is the guidance in this?"

Now she was having the same old smile at the very first beginning when she said she doesn't like her job she said

"I got into education industry cause I really want to be a teacher initially, I really wanted to be something that could help students for their education, but the administration of these coaching institutes have made so many compulsions that even I am not sure what should I be doing now to earn my living I am into this industry from last 15 years and my job is not the counselling my job is to trap the parents of the students, no matter what the students can do, what are his qualifications, the student belongs to this industry or not, and to take parents into confidence we are having so many tests as well most of them are just is fake as the picture of some students hanging on the wall, and if I refuse to do so the management is not going to pay me, this education is somehow made into a kind a business where they are going to earn from a topper whether the topper is from there institute or not, whether they teach them or not, they pay the toppers to earn from them, and they are earning money from the failures as well, and that is why I said at the very beginning I don't like my job I feel like I am cheating"

I asked her

"I have to say, I agree with you are right here but if this is the situation here at your institute then why don't you change you should change the institute, and you should shift at a better institute where you will not feel like this"

Now she laughed a little and said

"That is so nice of you Rahul but don't you think this thought is something I didn't get before, in the last 15 years I have been almost every institute around the city, and our city is having centers of almost all the brands which are into this industry, and I am not able to find one brand or one institute which doesn't do like this, never I get to interview they ask me the number of parents I can convince for the admission, how will I convince them, even the training and everything they have is overall for the admission of a student, I really wish there could be a better situation for this system, but at this stage it feels like everything is out of my hand"

> "If one speaks with a pure mind, happiness follows like a shadow."
>
> \- Buddha

Finding dishonesty isn't that typical around us, but even if the situation is like this, we have to solve it. We all are going to be a part of this society and it's our responsibility to make it better. I am talking about the biggest part of your universe here, and that is you.

So let's talk about a solution oriented approach here, if we know how much honesty is important, then we should be teaching it to our kids as well right? Let's find out. Let's try to understand the aspect from an example, in Japan there is no housekeeping staff there, hospitality staff, actually the cleaning of classrooms, halls and the whole school is done by all the teachers students and even principal also do the cleaning. Can you imagine how effective this can be, not just a sign of humbleness, a way more than that. There is a line.

"Kids don't do what you say. They do what they see. How you live your life is their example."

- Tim Ferriss

I often see that parents complain that my kids lie often, have you ever wondered what teacher in the world will teach students how to lie? Or even a parent who is teaching their kids to lie? No you won't be able to find one. May be at the later stages of life. But during education, there won't be any.

So from where they start to learn how to be dishonest? A father is playing with his kid, suddenly his boss calls, and asks,

"Where are you now?"

He says,

"Sir I can't come to office, as I am out of town." Or

"Sir, I am suffering from fever." Or

"Sir, I am having a medical emergency at family."

One what we say becomes our life, so we should be very careful about what we are saying, two this is where the kid learns, that it is okay to tell a small lie for what we love to do. And this "Love to do" becomes a huge variation in definition later on as well. Similar things you will be noticing with ladies as well. I have observed many times that mother is talking to another female neighbor. And while talking they talk bad about anybody else who isn't present that time.

"I had doubt on her character from the beginning."

"I wish she wouldn't have come to our society."

"These people are spoiling the peace of ours too."

"I just don't want to see her again in my life."

And if once that same person comes to home, they pretend as if they are very good friend of them, and behaves as if there is nothing bad inside.

They sometimes even get confused over it, over our behavior too, that mother was abusing this lady before an hour, and now behaving as if she is my best friend. What's wrong here? Even sometimes they stop in middle of these type of discussion when they learn from anywhere else that we should not talk bad.

I often hear this from kid trying to teach parents that mother we should not use bad words, then mother herself convince their own kids by saying,

"We are just talking."

"We are not saying anything bad about anything, it's true"

Sometimes I even see parent's scolding their own kids in front of the other person too.

"Good kids don't interrupt in elder's talk."

"Kid go and complete your homework, you should study."

Even if you will look closely, you will be able to see parents that mother or father usually using mobile phones, and asks their kids to go and do their study or homework. Is that kid going to do study? They may not even get interest in studies, sometimes they even gets back to parents or elders.

"You are using mobile for an hour, and not letting me to use for 10 minutes only."

"I never saw you reading and you always asks me to study."

"You complain a lot about everything, and asks me not to complain about."

Even there are so many jokes too, representing the same aspect.

"Papa is saying that he is not at home."

"Mamma doesn't like you, that's why she doesn't want to talk to you. But she will call you back, she said."

"My theory is children don't do what you tell them to do, they do what you do. You have to always do the right thing because they follow you."

- Boman Irani

This phenomenon is something which is easily visible if you will try to see so.

Where the leader of the country is honest, People are usually honest.

If the Parents in the family are honest, so the kids become too.

If the school's management, administration is honest, so the teachers will become, and so the students will become too.

Vice versa is true too.

If father takes alcohol often, kids will also begin earlier.

If parents smokes, than children will begin earlier.

If parents fights often, you won't be able to find peaceful children there.

Logic is very simple, whatever we are going to do, is going to return through us, under the same roof of ours. If we treat everyone humbly, then a humbleness is something which will fill our life with happiness. If we honest, honesty is surely a byproduct, and you will feel it. But if we are cheating people, get ready to be cheated. If we are doing anything bad by any means, we should be ready for same too.

Don't watch soap operas if you don't want your kids to watch these, Instead read good books, if you want your kids to study, don't play mobile games often if you don't want your kids to play the same. Don't lie if you don't want your kids to lie. Do the best and expect the best.

Very similar thing is with the school as well, at the time of annual function most of the schools try to show their achievements to parents, they even hang every of their achievements on the reception area.

And when a kid starts showing his achievements, they may say showing off isn't a good thing kid, we should not show off our achievements. Then in the same assembly they are going to do the same.

"Be the change you want to see in the world."

- Mahatma Gandhi

I remember a story of a person travelling in the bus, he had two kids and a wife with him, the person didn't seem to be rich, a lower middle class attire, the bus conductor welcomed him, and gave him three tickets, and asked.

"Please take your seat sir."

The person stopped there, and asked the conductor

"I need four tickets not three."

The conductor with a confused look, said

"Sir the bus is free for the kids below age 4."

The person said with a smile.

"I know, my daughter in my hand is 4 years and 3 months now."

The conductor got impressed, and said with his wide eyes and smile.

"Sir, if you won't have said, I wouldn't have known, so it doesn't matter."

But what the person said is still in my ears.

"You wouldn't have known the fact, but my family would have known what kind of person I am."

The solution is sincerely simple, don't ask your kids to do anything, instead take the hard way, and do what you want them to do. For a mother if you want your kid to watch soap operas, or some social media videos all the time, then only do these. But if you want your kid to read, start reading right now.

If you want your kid to play games outside, go with them play outside.

If you want your kid to be hard working, don't sit on couches or bed often, work hard!

If you want your kids to be Honest. Be HONEST.

"Honesty is not a quality, a person should have. It's a necessity."

- Rahul Bajad

Necessity 6

Social Animal

"STOP SAYING, PEOPLE DON'T OWE EACH OTHER ANYTHING!!

We owe each other community.

We owe each other love.

We owe each other safety.

We owe each other support.

Individualism is destroying us."

- Audra

Remember when we were kids, we were unable to speak, but our parents and elders were knowing how to speak. All of them were always so busy in making us understand how to speak, they always try to make us speak. It was a never ending process.

If I ask you a simple question, how come you know that the thing in your hand is a book? You know it because somebody told you this

"That the structure of these set of pages, written printed or drawing" or

"A medium to store information", or

So many definitions available of a book too. These definitions are the way we know that this thing in our hand is a book, right?

But this is overall a definition made by somebody to ease the understanding of ours, this is how everything was introduced. We know about each and everything because of our surroundings. This society teaches us a lot. And in this society almost no one has got bad intentions of teaching us anything. Everyone has got good intentions, and with these good intentions only, they try to introduce us to something or show us something.

"We owe our children – the most vulnerable citizens in any society – a life free from violence and fear."

- Nelson Mandela

You are going to hear this often that you could have good intentions but you won't be able to do well no matter how hard you try. Well there are so many reasons for that why people say so. Almost everybody who are into education or who are studying overall they always want to be a good person and want to have good intentions but something happens in between and the drop being good anymore. It is a similar kind of methodology of giving up there was a line that in a negative environment positive person face trouble, and vice Versa is also true that in a positive environment and negative person faces troubles. Most of the things happened because of environment.

There is a Bollywood movie based on a true story, you can even find on IMDB.com, named 12th fail. Right now the stories on second rank. The story is based on true characters and the main character there belongs to my own state. His name is Manoj Kumar Sharma. I was watching an interview of him, in which he was overall saying, that he struggled for years and everybody is appreciating his story of a struggle and finally he became a powerful officer. But even after becoming the officer the villagers around us village, the people in his neighbourhoods were saying to their family and other people, that we are not going to teach our kids to become like Manoj because even after struggling of more than 15 years, and one she got the position of an officer, you are supposed to be successful, but he has not made a big home, neither he is buying a good car, nor he is rich. So what is the use of this success, we don't want this success.

After making this kind of statement even the officer who was being interviewed, he said that this mentality of comparison success to richness is dangerous and that is what it is creating trouble all around the society and world. We all are social animals, we should be serving back in thanks, and this comparison is the evil here. Even he said to his wife as well I always want to be an honest officer and I want your help in that, will it do for you if you will not wear gold or diamond or these kind of jewelleries are the things which are being considered as status symbol over here which actually are not.

He also said that my wife and I never supports these kinds of status symbols, all those words for a little different and of course the interview was in Hindi language but what I am trying to say here we all want our kids to be successful, and with that we want our kid to be rich. This comparison of success and richness create a kind a confusion in the mind of a student as well as society. The people who are rich no matter how they have earn money people consider them successful this philosophy has to be changed.

"Successful people have a social responsibility to make the world a better place and not just take from it."

- Carrie Underwood

There are hundreds of reasons why it has to be changed but even it will be able to work on any of it. The purpose of making his book will be solved.

Before getting to it we should be knowing about success, what is success? The definition of success is again different from the perspective of person to person. And this different definition is creating a whole dilemma over here in our society. Let me ask you the same thing, what is success according to you?

You must have a good definition of success but to get the actual meaning of success we must have the true meaning of success in our mind as well, let's get to basic. A person is considered to be successful if he gets what he wants. And this is why the definition varies from person to person. Because everybody want different things. As an example somebody is wanting to have a big car, if he gets the car, the same car he was wanting, then we can call him a successful person in achieving his car, and we can call this success. Another example is suppose I want a burger, and I get the same burger, so I am successful in getting a burger, that's it. Success overall mean nothing else.

Success overall depends upon the goal of yours what do you actually want. What should I be saying you can get successful every day? There can be small success there can be big success. But whole dilemma of sadness begins with the comparison, when the person who was wanting something starts comparing his success to somebody else's words. Let's take and begin from a small example, one person wants a burger and another person wants a pizza. Both gets what they want, the first one is getting a burger, and the second one is getting a pizza. The both are successful overall, but now the issue happens, they starts talking to each other about their success. The first person believes the second person is unsuccessful, because the second person didn't get the burger. Weird thing is second person may think the same for the first person. And opposite happens too. They starts doubting themselves maybe I am not successful, the other person is successful. And this whole dilemma makes the society a bad place to live. And weird thing is through all of us.

"There is no definition of success, Everyone's success is different. You can't compare your success to someone else's."

- Anonymous

You can replace the burger and pizza with anything, say 1 million bucks, 2 million bucks, a big car, a big home, a happy family, a publicity stunt, an activity of respect, it could be anything. And by replacing these things people behaves so weird. It begins with anything and it ends with anything, this comparison is having a huge variety. It begins with the first steps of walk. This kid is successful, as he started walking in couple of months, he successful he started talking, he started walking earlier than the neighbourhoods child, he started talking early at then my sister's kid. And the whole dilemma begins, the education system, the society, everybody begins this game with everything. He gets better marks on the subjects than him, he is better in football than anybody, somebody is better at chess, somebody is better at communication, somebody is better at languages, now somebody is earning good, somebody is having big car, somebody is having big house, somebody is having big family, somebody is happy, somebody's happier than somebody, somebody is being respected more, and this comparison of somebody to somebody never stops, from one brother to another, from one family to another, from one home to another, from one Street to another, from one district to another, from one City to another, from one state to another, from one country to another, from one continent to another, from one planet to another, even from one solar system to another, from one almighty to another, and trust me they are willing to even kill each other on the name of this comparison.

And if I have to tell you about the true meaning of comparison and if you would look at it a little more carefully, it is one of the most dangerous thing humans have created. Let me show you how, suppose there are two people are getting compared from birth on their perspective of success, one started to walk a little earlier than other. And most of the people will compare in between the two and the statement is going to say is, one walked earlier. And here the word earlier is what creating the whole bad of a situation. This word earlier is a comparative word, once we use this we compare something with something. And this overall comparison says which is better and which is not. It is a kind of competition, which one is better which one is not. And the bad most thing about the competition is somebody has to lose. So the one who started walking early won, and the one who started walking a little late loses.

And this competition begins with everything sometimes the one who started walk later may starts to talk earlier. Now the situation changes and the one who talked earlier is the person who won. In this same scenario the whole life, they are going to compete with each other. Sometimes the first one wins sometimes the second one and till their death this is not going to stop. People will compare even after the death. That this funeral was better than him. Just thought process is ridiculous. Because this competition is the never ending process.

If two people are competing with each other, or two groups, this could be of anything, could be of a street, a city, any religion, any home, money, could relate with things, no matter what they are completing on the bad most thing is one has to lose. Do you know what happens to the person who loses? Now this person gets a feeling and hear a desire gets up. His initial feeling is very bad often. She feels disgusting, almost nobody celebrates the days of defeat. They are going to plan one more time to win from the same person. And in this process they pressurize themselves, they almost torture themselves to win from that another person. Sometimes this works sometimes this doesn't, now the person who loses previously is having a very bad feeling into him, may feel great when he wins, but when he will win the other person is going to lose. So to get a feeling of goodness into him, the person who loses works really hard and almost spoils all the days of his life to get one day of success. What kind of transaction is this? I have seen many people paying the price of day’s month’s years and even the pay their whole life in the mean of this competition to get one single day of happiness and respect.

And this same thing continues in our education system as well take the example of marks, in sports, in any indoor or outdoor activity. There is first second third and they are making per sentence out of it that you are at 92% you are at 91% you are at 93% you are a 50% this is this is something which is making a seed of competition into the child's brain.

"Comparing yourself to others does nothing for you. Society has conditioned us to value people who fit a secular mold of perfection."

- Michele Woolley

The result of this comparison methodology is disaster, the world has started comparing without even thinking. It harms the society. The harms of this comparison is limitless. One of the top worst most side effect of comparison is the effect on life. I got to study a criminal case of dowry. This dowry is something which was one of the evil in India. For those who don't know the dowry, and if I have to introduce it dowry is money given by father of bride to groom. People asks lakhs, crores of money for marrying their son as groom. It is a famous topic though. But let's try to get a thing I am trying to explain to you. The thing which can create a good effect in our society as well.

I got to meet a father who has made a case of dowry and was crying in front of me. He was saying that his daughter has been killed by couple of people who are living in that village nearby my city. For the very first moment I asked

"What happened?"

Her father said while he was crying

"My daughter was in so much pain, they were continuously asking for money from me, I have already told them I do not have much money but they do that often, and the killed my daughter finally when I couldn't give them money, I have filed criminal case against her husband, and her husband was in jail from more than one and half year, I want that person to face what he did, I have lost my daughter, and so I want justice, I want them to feel they did wrong"

"When we live in a false society, that bases its wealth upon money, then that society itself will collapse eventually. Not because I say so, because it's not based on physical reference."

- Jacque Fresco

With this very first statement of father I felt as if,

Why will a person ask for dowry?

How much money they need?

Why to do so?

What will they do with this much money?

I had so many questions and I was extremely angry with those idiots good took life of his daughter. They were villages the people who filed the case were also, the people who are facing this case were also. I got chance to visit father's family, he was genuinely not rich and was having five daughters, I asked him

"Why did you have five daughters if you could not make their living by yourself?"

He said

"I need somebody as son, who would carry my precious name of my ancestors as well further"

In India too we have got this rules that after marriage girls name will be changed and her surname will be named after her husband surname. I didn't like that that 6 kids were something he had, and he had them even after knowing that he is poor he won't be able to make their living. This thought process has also come from the comparison methodology and the teachings learnings from the ancestors, of course there are so many things responsible for this thought process, but my main concern over here was his daughter is dead and I get to know that has daughter was having two more daughters.

I was initially feeling that if I will be getting a chance I would have taught a lesson to that groom, to all of his family that

Why did they do this, for money?

Is money is something more important than somebody's life?

They were taking me as an educated person initially, and they were wanting me to help them. And I thought maybe I should try to help them, of course I am not judge here so I thought let's first understand the things why did they do that.

With a friend of mine and grooms in common i went to that grooms place, just to know couple more things. When I went there I came to know they are rich people. They were having two cars with them, a big bungalow, a big joint family, plenty of space for all the people to live together, and plenty of money they had. They were not knowing why did I came. So they behaved very well with me. I met two of the daughters of the girl who died. The two girls were playing with their grandfather, the grooms father, I should be saying. My first thought on them was they are bad people and doing bad. They might be pretending to be good.

I must be saying and I could say this to you as well,

"Never consider the statement of a person whose standing at the bank of rivers how the water is. The person who is already swimming into it, is already deep into it can only give you a better suggestion of how the water is actually."

\- Rahul Bajad

So after taking a breakfast over there, I have decided to meet couple more people in the neighbourhoods, and was willing to ask them how the groom's family actually is. A weird thing happened that day out of 6 neighbourhoods homes no one said even a single bad thing about them, they all were appreciating them instead. They all were having good stories about them, most of them we are saying they are very generous people they help so many villages around, Very social and helping. And one person in the neighbourhoods was very sure, and said

"A very bad suicide case happened in their family, the bride was having two children after her she should not be committing suicide. Comparing a village life with a city life has become dangerous for the life of those two kids who does not have a mother, and only able to see father in jail"

I didn't understand it completely, but one thing was pretty sure about it there is something I don't know, both of the parties were sounding good. Both seem generous, both have got their own points, but Dowry was still something I sincerely hate. So I couldn't stop myself in getting a little deeper towards it. So after a month I decided that my holiday should be spent on the truth because the two children were not having neither mother nor father. I really wanted to do something for them. So I went to the advocate who as fighting the case of that groom, children's fathers. When I got to him, and asked the same question, he smiled at me. After that smile, he forwarded one diary to me.

That diary took my soul out of my body. That diary was of that father who was in jail from last one and half year, Advocate sir later said that do match the words, this diary is written by the groom himself, and take your own honest judgement. I wish I could say it as it is, there were more than 60 pages overall, but the powerful truth I came to know were so powerful.

Truth number 1, the groom loved his wife a lot, way more than even expected by even girl's father, there were so many things he mentioned in the book, of course he wasn't a writer, but in his own words he mentioned one incident, that the wife was once asked for one coconut water to drink, the groom bought the whole street shop of coconuts, and filled his whole car with those, to give those to his wife, was trying to make her happy, and he was successful, better one he did is, he got scolded by his parents for this mischievous act, and those coconuts were something had to shared.

He also mentioned another story of mobile phone bill, they used to talk before marriage, that once the mobile phone bill was more than, half of his monthly income that month. After reading these, I felt like, if they were in love, why will he or his father will ask for money. I thought may be groom's father or mother be greedy. But then I came closer to a line, he wrote. That line was,

"If we were wanting dowry from her parents, then why will we ever marry in that Samaj Sammelan, those people are not even ashamed of the fact, that coz of her own sister, she killed herself."

The "samaj sammelan" could be a term you might not be knowing. It is a kind of marriage usually organized by some NGOs (Non-Government Organizations) or any person who just want to help poor people for marriage, especially in the case, if the girl's father is not capable enough to bear the cost of marriage or dowry.

Now this fact, took all of my focus, and even I saw the pictures of the marriage, those, I saw the home of girl's father, he was poor I came to know that. Later I saw the home of the groom too, he was a comparatively rich fella, lived in joint family, had 2 cars, a small bungalow, big place for farming, and their main business was milk dairy. Now so many questions were popping in my head. Is it a suicide or the people killed because of dowry, who is lying here?

Then I came closer to that report from the medical department, who confirmed that the reason death is the rope, she hanged her with. Now the people at the bride's side, her father, her family and then I saw her sister one day. Now the groom got out of jail on bail. I was able to talk to him as well. These two new characters were in my sight, of course I am not judge here, but I knew for sure there is something wrong has happened, and the two kids lost their mother. I went to the bride's family. I saw something really weird. Bride's sister, was elder sister of hers, now this lady, was having a world of different personality than the one who committed suicide. I was thinking this much difference in two sisters. She was initially talking in an educated manner. Her dress was something comparatively modern than the village girls, not like her passed sister. And her husband was also wearing educated clothes, educated accent. I felt like these two educated people can tell me what actual reason of this dilemma is.

I got to them, and as I was close to bride's family, the person playing role of bride's sister's husband admitted the fact. That the case is not of dowry. He was blaming something else now. I felt as if, from the very first day I am seeing this as a case dowry as the bride's father was saying. Now this person admitted more, that bride's father knows nothing, he barely got to talk to her, he doesn't had even money to get his daughter to the hospital, and the bride usually and rarely go to her parents too. Now this was more confusing, and I asked then why her father is saying so, and this person also admitted because me and my friend, who was also the advocate from the bride's side, he said so. Now this was something I didn't like. I asked that person, then why are you doing this, and he replied,

"These people were all bad to the bride."

This reply was not good enough for me.

I had so many questions, if the groom's parents and groom were not greedy, and the blame is they took the life because of greediness than what could it possibly be. Initially I was into it because, bride's father was considering me an educated person to help, but now I was just able to think about the two children, looking for their mother, so I didn't stop here, I again convinced my friend and we both went to the groom's family, I saw groom was playing with his both children, and got a chance to talk to him, I took the chance and tried to talk with him, face to face. As he was one of the closest one to bride. Now the picture got way clearer from here.

The groom, was getting so emotional with these questions, and when I asked him

"Brother if the issue of her death is not dowry, then what is the reason that she decided to take her own life"

He answered

"Maybe it's my fault brother, I couldn't choose in between her and my parents."

His tears this time was not saying as if he was lying, but still, I was willing to know the truth in a better way that I could understand it from my perspective. I said

"I didn't get you brother, what happened?"

Now he smiled and shown me couple of messages of bride on his cell phone, messages were of more than of 7 and 8 months from the day she killed herself. Let's get to the messages later to get better understanding, I asked him another question.

"Brother the messages you have mainly saying that the argument, your issue happened after 2 years of your marriage, was everything okay for 2 years"

He answered

"Yes brother everything was going fine, I am not sure what exactly happened."

So I asked him again

"When it all was started."

He said

"It all started after 2 years of my marriage, it was her sister's marriage anniversary, and we both were called to her home in city, we went there, and after a week and so, she often was willing to go to her sister's home in city, so we used to go to meet her once, and then twice a month, we were having a good time there, but at my home, it all was becoming difficult for me and my kids to survive"

Isn't you wondering how, this is relating? The message what he got to me were saying like. The wife was saying to his husband.

"My love, why can't we go to city and live there only? Why do we have to live in the village only? Let's make our career and life in city"

And the husband was saying

"My whole business is here, my family is here, everything through which we are making our living is here, how will I be able to leave everything."

And this choice continued for 7 months, and the last time she communicated was that,

"I don't want to have this life, after me please take care of our kids, I wish we could live a better life in city, like my sister, but this life here in village, I cannot take it anymore, good bye my love, please take care of our kids."

Now the whole picture was almost clear, I asked the husband,

"Brother, why was she wanting to live in city? Didn't you both like all here for 2 years?"

Husband replied

“Everything was going great here, we have got two child’s, everything was going good, we had everything, complete family, money, successful business, happy parents, happy family, I couldn’t have asked for more, we all were content, then after visiting her sister’s, she was never content, and I was trying my whole life to make her content and happy, but I failed, I am partially responsible for this, maybe I should have gone to city, her sister had seen a place for use to buy and live there, she even had plans for business for us, what else can be done, they were not living with their parents, city life, freedom was there, maids were there, facilities were there, maybe I should have shifted, if I would have my kids could have mother”

“Success is not about being ahead of others, failure is not being behind. Comparison never gives anything but takes away the peach of mind.”

- With Bhawna Gautam

After two months in court, the husband was trying to convince them to take the case back, and was saying

“Either take the children with you, or please let me do the parenting.”

And her sister’s family including her sister’s husband were saying

"You didn't listen to us, we won't forgive you, and you took the life of my sister"

My sister, my daughter, or what so ever that relation was.

This husband person was feeling guilty for it, and he was not that educated either. The bride's father, he was not that educated either, he was also feeling guilty, and I should never have married my daughter to this bad person. The two people who were educated, from their perspective, they were trying to do something nice to her sister, and was trying to make village people more modern, more educated, and more future oriented.

"Comparing yourself with others is one of the highest forms of self-destruction and people who love themselves don't destroy themselves."

- Sarvesh Jain

If we see closely, almost everyone were having good intentions, but the whole court case was all fake. Everyone, including bride, groom, their families, even, sisters had good intentions, but a big but was.

The father of two children, the husband was suffering.

Bride, wife was suffering, and is no longer available.

The whole family who were having bond together were suffering.

From the groom's side too,

From the bride's side too.

The least suffer was there for the two children no, it's been more than a year, both kids were playing even in the court room.

Definitely you and I both have rights to make the opinions. I am not sure about your opinion, though you should also have one, but from my opinion, Look guys, bad is happened for sure, but bad intentions are very difficult to find. But bad is happened right, this is worst actually, and from my opinion what took the life of mother of two kids, there are so many things and so many people from my perspective. And in that list, few top most are...

1. We have lost the true meaning of what we are in actual for us and society.
2. Success has got much diversified meaning we have to understand.
3. This comparison methodology through success of one another is weird most, if success is different for everyone, than how can it be compared?
4. Comparing village life to city life, ridiculous.
5. She was content until she didn't see the city's shine.
6. Non educated people thought process that they are less than educated one.

7. Educated people's thought process that they are better.
8. Lost true meaning of education.
9. Lost true values of Morals.
10. Ego is bigger killer than weapon. As it was there too
11. How even love can be dangerous.
12. And above all, everybody is lying to themselves that they all were concerned about the life of the two children's who lost their mother.

"Comparison is the thief of joy"

- Theodore Roosevelt

Let's get to a solution oriented approach here, take an example of finland here again, it has got 100% literacy rate here, no comparison with the village or city, no comparison with the men women, gender inequality, rich or poor, almost for now, the whole nation without comparison to it is like a family, no one is illiterate or no one is discriminated or feels like different through education. Look at like this. We owe a lot to society but before that, Let me ask you one simple question, is an apple better than rose? Come on think again, is an apple better than a rose? Let's twist it, is a rose is better than an apple? I asked it thrice because I actually want you to think about it. There is no comparison with any of it.

Suppose right now, right here, our almighty listens to us, and our almighty takes every different thing from everyone, and make everything best, imagine it like this, everyone is a billionaire now, everyone has got so many cloths, everybody is rich, everybody is physically powerful, let's take it to another level, every person has got same skin tone, same diet, same food, same face, same character, it seems more like whims and fancies. Face the truth my friends, if there is light everywhere, then the light is nowhere, if there is darkness everywhere, then there is no darkness, people are going to even going to recognize if there was a thing named light. The beauty of this world is all our uniqueness, if everyone is rich, it means no body is rich. Everybody is all same. And if everybody is exactly the same, then this is not world. Is it something needs explanation?

This is the issue with comparison, it only and only creates unhappiness, if the almighty would have given chance to me, I could have deleted all the comparative words out of dictionary, he is small, he is big, he is fat, he is thin, he is bad, he is good, these all are almost all of them are being used in the sense of unhappiness. Discontentment is the child of comparison. You tell me, out of 87lakhs of species, we humans are the only one who compares. And this dis contentment is sticks with us only coz of that. Can't we appreciate what we have? And we have got plenty take my words with this. 25000 people die daily because of hunger, out of which 15000 are kids. Tell me one this the lady who decided to suicide, was she not having food in her plate of her choice? Was she not having cloths, roof and shelter, she was having a four wheeler machine at her home, a bungalow, fresh air, respect around the village. Wasn't it enough for her, and for others too, who even thinks of ending the life. She was happy initially when she was content, and she was content this was the main reason she was happy. The moment she compared, that was the same moment, her life became measurable, and if something is taking our happiness, how in the can that thing be good.

What do you think, what matters the most? Is being into educated people is this much important? Or the education itself is? If this what the meaning of education is spreading in the whole society than this is something which has to be stopped by us too. The true meaning of education can be anything but this? I really don't think so. This is actually why I want you all to know and understand it, than please be educated you should and you have right to, but get a clear meaning of education first in your mind. Once you will see the true meaning of education into it, than you will find it as a gem.

"You leave home to seek your fortune and, when you get it, you go home and share it with your family"

- Anita Baker

Secondly there was one more person who was having difficulties in understanding meaning of education and it's fortune, we all are comparing ourselves with what we are not, we want to eat like the other people, we want to wear like the other people, we want to live like the other people, and by this other people everyone who pretends and shows off their so called useless achievements.

Let's take example, first, does everyone want to leave their parents willingly? If they are willingly wanting to leave their parents, then getting success into it, this could be an achievement, but from their perspective only. Almost every successful person in the world whom so ever is being considered as successful by the whole world are either having their parents with them, happily. This is one of the parameter of success, why do we have to wait for a festival to come? As the reason of getting a chance to spend some time together? Out of both sisters, with this parameter, who was more successful? Off Couse the one who was living in village.

"Any success you achieve at the expense of your family is not real success."

- Davewills.org

Second example, having one successful business is more successful? Or having a job of somebody else is considered as more successful? With no offense to job people too, but even the statistics says, I read one day that statistics says, only 15% are engaged at their job, rest 85% are unhappy at it. So in this contrasting nature too, who was more successful, off course the one in the village.

Let's talk about the family now, if the girl who was willing to live their life in city and her sister who was already in city, both were having kids, this village lady had to leave their kids to somebody else, in that case also they had to leave the family, and can anybody be happy without family again. What is the use of job and career, if we follow the statistics, finding a good job, is as difficult as finding the right partner. But on the cost of leaving two infants? What kind of success was there in city in that case? I am not able to find any, I am not against of making a career, having dreams or something, but if 85% of the people are unhappy, and saying that I am doing job because it is my dream, some pretty bad lines like, "if the destination is beautiful, don't care about the path". It is not a forest walk my friend, it is life, and the birth of human is not made to be unhappy. It is like insulting the life in itself.

The educated sister, who might be wearing makeup, might be wearing modern cloths, might be bold at communication comparatively, but every educated person, at least who believes I am educated, they should not pretend as if everything is best in their life, if they don't love their education, if they don't love what they are doing at job, if they hate their bosses. Then I believe, after drinking a poison, and making his own life measurable at anything, how can a person, a father, an elder brother, a mother, or anyone could even ask next generation to drink it, by saying, everybody has done this, and you have to do the same my son. Suppose if the person who made the education system is questioned the same.

Is this is what the educated people you were imagining, then the answer is a BIG NO!

Is this what the education system is designed to make?

So my friend, there is something wrong happening around the world. And we have to fix it.

That fix is with the practical solution to this, this is here. A possible one would be. Imagine with me like this,

A school which has a minimum fees structure or free. A structure what a poor most man could also bear. Not allowed for any business tycoons to make it a business.

A school where dresses will be provided to all by the school only same dress same bag, same books, same compass box, same pencil and copies even, an equal conveyance may be, same on very reasonable ones. Again a government contract or some good NGO's work included no business here too.

Few countries are doing so, the best part of this system is, if everyone has got a same bag, so there won't be any comparison in the children, there will be same pencil compass, and there won't be any comparison with the valuables. No poor kid will feel as if he is poor. No rich kid would feel as if he is rich.

Take example of Finland Privatization is banned there in schooling, not just that Finland is considered to be the most powerful education system in the world. I understand we are having a huge population so the concept is not that doable. But what If we can do something good at least with our kid to follow some of the protocols. At least we can understand that comparison is a dangerous virus spoiling the whole society.

If you would want a family to be, what kind of family you would want. They all should have respect for each other. Should have love for each other, we owe this to society too. Let's create a better place to live. It should be the part of education. And the education begins from the beginning of learning. So it's not necessarily the responsibility of school but of ours too. For our family and ourselves.

"Society is family, and a family isn't just made to give love, it is responsibility too, isn't escapable, It has to be done, sooner or later, so let's do it with love."

- Rahul Bajad

Necessity 7

Responsibility

"If you realise your responsibility, you will realise your destiny."

- Tasneem Hameed

People often get confused with the two terms guru and teacher, both may seem the same, but both are not, if I should be talking about the definition the word guru is a combination of two words "gu" and "ru". The word "Gu" means darkness or dark, and the word "ru" means lightness or light, the word guru overall means the power that takes us from gu to ru, from dark to light. This is where a vision comes into picture. You can understand through this a guru is somebody who overall helps in vision, in enlightening the path. So, if a person is somehow misleading or helping in this bad deed can't be considered a guru for sure.

In a contrasting way the word teacher is basically for a person who teaches, and to teach means to give lessons or instructions. I have used word contrasting here because both of the words are very different from each other. But what if I ask you that are these teachers having intentions not to teach? But is there something which is not letting them do so?

"Where there is no vision, there is no hope."

- George Washington Carver

I got a chance to work with an art teacher, who used to teach senior students too. She was checking some drawings from a class, and she had more than 500 drawings to check through. The time was something 9 pm here, and the family and me somehow waiting for her to have dinner. When I saw she was so busy with her work,

I asked her

"Aren't your work timings from 7 am to 3 pm?"

My words fell on his heart as if she found somebody who understood their issues at their job. She replied wholeheartedly

"Yes, you are right, the timings are from 7 am to 3 pm but we often have to take care of the other words than teaching from home".

"Seriously often? For example,"

I asked. She spoke

"Apart from teaching I have got so many responsibilities at the school, like a free managed period's arrangements, being called on school even at school is on off, that time too some kind of other work is being given by them, they don't allow us to check copies often at this time, above it as during the time of annual function I have to design the stage, make all the props for the performances, need to create rangolis all around the school, have to decorate the school, there is no extra time or extra payment for that, and they want us to do all of these altogether",

She was saying all these as if a volcano has burst out, I was staring her with a shocked look, how used to her is getting of these works, and while talking with me, she was able to check copies and drawings too, she continued

"With all these responsibilities, we are supposed to take care of family, kids, in laws, have to make food for all of them, and have to make time for ourselves too",

As I was close to that family, I couldn't stop myself asking

"Is there anything I can help you with here?"

You will be amazed too at what I came to know then, she said

"Rahul you can check the drawings for me",
Now this was not understandable. I asked her with curiosity as well as in a shocked way

"How can I check the copies of your students? you know what you may have taught them, what they have made for you, it's you who gave them tasks and they worked hard for these drawings to get good marks here right?",

Her mood instantly changed, she got a little happy with my question and replied

"Rahul don't worry about it, no one in the whole society cares about it, all you have to do is take these all drawings make a right sign, with this red pen, and if you like any drawing just give them A, if don't like much give them B, it's easy!"

This was getting interesting, I was amazed by, and couldn't stop myself saying

"You are playing with the future of students" the next line was more shocking what she replied,

"Who me? Every teacher in the school, every teacher in other schools is suffering with similar pain as I do, almost every teacher is checking copies or working in the schools the same way I do."

Her answer still dances in my head. And it was not the situation of that lady only, it was, and it is the situation of all the teachers and education staff who are called teachers.

"There are two primary choices in life: to accept conditions as they exist, or accept the responsibility for changing them."

- Denis Waitley

She was having problems but the answer to the problem was not visible even to a far distance. In that perspective, the grades are worthless for sure. If a student is spending hours creating a drawing, and a teacher is not having a minute to see it properly, the teacher will never be able to answer the question of what has to be done for the student to be better. And this thing will go on and on. Try to look at the things around you too, if a kid is drawing badly and has this topic of drawing in schools for at least 10 years, 10 years of drawing periods he is in, and the drawing progress and difference in elder's drawing and a kid's drawing is minute the kids are drawing the heart of them, and an elder in place of kids lost that emotion too. Growth and betterment of the drawing are negligible. And it feels bad to say that here too, the situation of drawing through such a teacher is very similar to all the subjects of all the students almost everywhere. You and I both know exceptions in students are there, and teachers are too. But most of the percent is falling in this category.

Come on, ask yourself that alpha, gamma, sine theta cos, theta, things we all have learned once, the bad we are at drawing in the same manner almost all of us are still bad at those terms and their knowledge too. Because almost we all did the same thing, the situation of every subject of ours in the perspective of knowledge is way worse than it used to be.

The topper of mathematics and topper of science in our class are still utilizing only 0.5% of all the knowledge they gained from school and college education. And they are utilizing most of their energy on some survival tricks.

"Knowledge without application is simply knowledge. Applying the knowledge to one's life is wisdom, and that is the ultimate virtue."

- Kasi Kaye Iliopoulos

Another example will surely help, with a suggestion, let me give you another, especially to parents and the readers too they can get to any of the loved ones. Never ever miss a chance to meet the teacher of your loved one. I am not the best father but always willing to be one for my kid. So I never miss a parents teachers meeting, this may sound crazy but I even requested CCTV footage for my kids first school days. I still have that. So the incident is of one of the parent's teachers meeting only, I met my son's another class teacher this time it was not an accident a very no so well planned but planned meeting.

She was his class teacher and there were around 40 students in class. The first greetings words were,

"Ooh hi! How's you today",

Seems promising, than she asked my son his name.

"What's your name bachaa (kid)?"

She didn't remember his name. And this destroys the first line of greeting's love too. The first one how's you today came out to be fake too. I thought okay this not a good start let's see how the middle one goes. When my son answered her question

"Mam, my name is Parv Bajad."

She was searching my son's test copies took a little time, I was clearly able to see her face how she was trying to find the copies of him where she might have kept it. She handed me all the copies and asked me to check them all in front of her in the classroom. And shown me the classroom. It was his classroom. My son said

"Papa this is my classroom, and I often sit here, let's sit at the same place",

I said

"No my love, let's sit at the back, we shouldn't disturb everyone here."

We both settled at the back of it.

There were so many pages there so I thought I won't be able to read them all, I opened the camera and started clicking pictures of his copies. I found the tries of his were cute and he is becoming a big boy there in school was always a fairy-tale, a key of happiness for me. So I wasn't focusing too much over his marks. He was just 8 years young and I always want him to be a good of him only that's it. And as I wasn't reading them my son was trying to show me his copies with excitement

"Look papa, here I got these many marks because I am good, here marks got cut I forget often, here mam scolded me so I forget, and here my friend was disturbing me so my writing was bad, but I got good marks at math's"

For me all of his words were like I am daydreaming. Suddenly I heard the same greetings for any other kid

"Ooh hi! How's you today?"

"What's your name bachaa (kid)?"

I felt bad, his class teacher was not able to remember any one's name. And I started to observe her. And tried to listen what she was saying.

She was behaving so mechanical same greetings, asking the name of student, seeing the marks of student. And through that marks she was saying some limited lines.

"Your son is bright student. Your daughter is not doing well, your daughter is good at mathematics, but she is not studying science."

She was pretending her best as if she knows every student very closely. But fake expressions were clearly and always visible like a fake smile. And you know what just like the smile when it is not genuine, if it is fake that it is irritating. I tried to dig up a little more and was trying to find out the answer why she is doing this. I settle there only for a while.

One parent was clicking the pictures of the same school copies she stopped them in middle and said

"Sir, clicking pictures of copies are not allowed here."

"Ohh okay okay that's my bad, I wasn't knowing it,"

That other parent said.

Now, I waited a little. Another teacher from another classroom came to her and she started sharing something

"This is going to be hectic yaar(friend), I got to meet more than 100's of parents my colleague didn't came today, I had to take care of her class also",

She replied

"Almost similar hectic situation is here too, checking copies preparing list of student's one list for administration, one list for parents, one for signatures, than list for marks, than trying to remember every student's name and record. There are more than 400 students of mine here friend, and few parents are very hard to handle"

They were a little far from us, and the parents in the front seats were not that so much capable to understand the English language, and she may have thought something similar about me too. Their voice were low but somehow if I could focus I can hear those all words very clearly.

I stood up after some time, and got to her with the copy. She again followed the same procedure, saw my son's marks told me the same thing what marks were saying, and then she told me a flat line,

"Your son intelligent and clever enough to focus on what he is looking for."

I heard that line previously too from her, so I didn't mind her. I signed there that I came to meet her, and I asked her

"Mam where can meet the other subject teachers?"

She told me a path to and arrangements of which subject teacher is which class's class teacher and where she might be. I got to meet every subject teacher that day. No teacher was able to remember my son's name, but everyone was having a similar complement for my kid a parent may want to hear. But I wasn't looking for that. I was looking for the reason that why these all are behaving like this.

As I said previously I am not judge, and tried to understand the situation here, and the situation is indeed hectic. As we got to know from the art teacher's story.

1. The additional works burden the administration is giving is not small.
2. They were not lying, they are professional subject teachers who's one period was of 45 minutes in each class of say 30 40 students.
3. There are more than 4 sections each class and suppose if she has 4 classes only to teach. She was

right, it is going 4x4 = 16 classes, 30 students per class that is 480 students she has to take care of.

4. If a person has to take care of more than 400 students how can she ever remember the name of students even in more than half of a year?
5. Above it, making exam papers for every class every section.
6. Have to submit test papers every month.
7. Have to submit attendance every day of students.
8. Checking copies of all the 400 students every week or month.
9. Syllabus is there.
10. Our parent's teacher meeting is there.
11. Staff meeting is there.
12. Mobile application update is there.
13. Now WhatsApp group management of students is there.
14. Every functions notification.
15. Material list.
16. Duty list.
17. Student's food's video.
18. Student's dance's video or classes reports to parents.
19. Annual day preparation 20. Festivals.
21. Student's diary,
22. The list is almost endless...

Even if the teachers are getting a little time to think in school that, what they should be doing to give student's a better education, the administration is not allowing them to be free. Even period arrangements are there.

But for this situation can a teacher be blamed or a management or administration has to be blamed? We should be talking a solution oriented discussion, there was a line

"The main thing is to keep the main thing the main thing."

-Stephen Covey.

In all these points and so called responsibilities the main education and its purpose is something which is very rare to find.

But with this there is another aspect that everything needs care, this care leads to management of things, they say getting to a peak of something isn't that hard as to maintain the same. To maintain and manage the education system smoothly there is definitely a big need of management.

But don't you believe the management is for the purpose of making things and system much better, and to maintain it in the similar or better stage. What if the situation is already poor and management and administration is trying to make it poorer or something worst, without having intentions to do something bad.

As we talked about intentions, it is not like that the intentions are always not the best, sometimes the intentions are best, but teachers have got high pressure to take of certain things along with education. The responsibilities given by administration. The so called system and the people who believe they are running the system. Teacher's wellbeing are concerned for so many countries, and they are very much important for us also to understand the importance of teachers too. If they will be happy then only our loved can be happy. So teachers should also be our loved ones.

"A good education system can change anyone. A good teacher can change everything."

\- Anonymous

Let's talk facts

- It is estimated that more than 1 in 5 teachers leave education in their first 3 years.
- An estimated 50% of teachers leave education within 5 years.
- 87% teachers state that work demands have interfered with family life.
- 45% teachers have considered leaving teaching due to standardized testing.
- 37% of the teachers who do not plan to teach until retirement site low pay being the reason. In india Low pay is one of the biggest reason quality educators are not taking interest in teaching too, that they won't be able to fulfil their family's requirements.
- Teacher's occupational stress is linked to student's phschological stress.
- 86% of the teachers state that they have insufficient planning time.
- Nearly 3 of 4 teachers report pressure to improve test scores.
- Teachers make 1500+ educational decisions a day on an average.

"Teacher's wellbeing is directly linked to the academic success of students."

\- Joyinteaching.com

This all is available on internet too. We can change this all.

So, now is the time for a solution oriented approach, there are certain things done at some powerful countries education systems to solve this issue of intentions of teachers, qualification of teachers, work pressure for them. Warning the idea may seem a little weird especially to those who are considering this education system is best.

Solution one, take example of India, according to right to education up to the age of 14 years is guaranteed as fundamental right under article 21A, of the constitution of India and a student can't be failed up to 8th class. If a child cannot be failed till 8th class, and if he is not doing well in exams, than what is the use of exams? And what if the kid is in class 3rd 4th, 5th or any other less than 8th, I agree that this may sound bad to most of the people. But again Finland doesn't have such policies. Before making any powerful statement, let me tell you this, Finland is considered to be the best education system if we go through google, you will find so many links saying so too.

1. They don't allow any kid to come to school before the age of 7, this mean the kid has to stay at home, learn through his own way, from parents, from family. Enjoy being a child instead of stuck with numbers, words and letters they prefer that it's not the age of a kid to put pressure of schools at them.

2. Even after the age of 7 they are not going to take any exams for next 6 years. The best thing even I appreciate this cause is, they are overall focusing over the learning of child, and they make sure that the child should learn more in comparison to any exam or education pressure. This concept seriously took my heart, let the kid be a kid first. This concept relives a lot of pressure from a child's head, not just him, but a teacher's mind can be free too, all they have to think about how the learning process is going in with the kids, they don't have to set an exam paper, no checking copies, no calling parents to come to meet for the exam papers checks, no functions has to be organized to keep every teacher and every staff busy for such PTM. Now with the right intentions teachers can definitely think a lot more about the child's education.

3. The same teacher concept. For 6 long years, the same teacher is going to teach students, they mean after the age of 7 to the next 6 years. Imagine like this, why a teacher is having hard time even remembering the kid's name? because children's are going to be changed every year, for the classes, one is teacher is going to spend their next 6 years with the same students, they will not just remember the name of child's they are going to remember so many things about the child, what he likes what he doesn't what he loves, what triggers his anger, how emotional he is, what is his learning capabilities, what are his interests at learning, this has got a lot,

a lot of possibilities, and is surely going to capture the possibilities into a child. In India we say "Disha sudharegi to dasha sudhregi", which mean once the direction improves, and situation improves.

4. A teacher is being considered as the most important asset to nation. Just like some powerful government posts too say IAS, IPS, exams like UPSC in India, they have got some similar criteria and examination. This mean everybody can't be a teacher a proper calibre measure is there. If the person deserves to be a teacher than only he will be selected and will be appointed by government officials for the job.
5. A sufficient salary is there for the sake of happiness of teacher, this way a huge reduction in the noise of complains from them too. I mean if I will be comparing this to similar education system nearby, the salary is comparatively too low for them and the perspective changes with it too. This aspect also solves so many problems. Specially affects attitude of teacher, and the people who are going to look at them.

"Everyone who remembers his own education remembers teachers. Not methods and techniques. The teacher is the heart of education system."

- Sidney hook

Bottom line what I am willing to tell is, If the person is financially good, mentally free, having precious emotions around, get attached to children's emotionally too, will be asked to teach students who are capable enough at least to understand things around. Say a kid of 7 years young and a kid of 3 years in age have got big of a difference in understanding of things. This whole process just not ease the job of a teacher, it eases the role of student too. And as a side effect of this. Children won't hate schools. It's like a web so many things are related with each other, dependent on each other. If the student is happy, he will have open mind, this mean he will understand it better, without pressure, they will try to learn things, not to mug things up. They will be emotionally connected with teachers and this gives a tremendous growth in the mind-set of kid. Will indeed make better humans and so as better society.

Let's tear these all apart, and not just put them in one paragraph. Which is extremely important too. But before that, I want you to do an activity here regarding the same process, I want you to take a minute and imagine your schooling or education place you are taking education from.

If you can remember please ask yourself these questions,

1. Was your teachers were having similar responsibilities and you may have thought they are not focusing on us properly?
2. What is the use of mugging these things?
3. Are they just trying to complete the syllabus?
4. Parent's teacher meeting pressure?
5. School administration pressure?
6. Issues with salary they may be facing?
7. Unable to maintain their own living?
8. Working as a teacher as if that was the last this he could do?
9. Teaching as compulsory work, not out of will, but out of compulsion?
10. Some teachers are good at intentions but lacking at skills?
11. Some are good at knowledge but unable to teach?
12. Some have well at teaching but they are not set free?

And the biggest of all these questions, Do we want our loved ones as new generations to face the similar issue with the education we have faced here? I know that talking about changing the system is not a piece of cake. But I remember a line, that

"If I won't be able to be a sun who enlighten the whole world. Then I will indeed become a street light bulb and will enlighten my street at the minimum."

If we will be able to change our mind-set at least and could understand the exact situation of education system and world. I am pretty sure we can together make a powerful world around us.

Trust me it's not just a responsibility of a teacher, but ours too,

Responsible persons create a responsible family,

Responsible families creates a responsible society,

Societies creates cities, cities creates nation, nations creates world.

It all begins with one and single one unit. It's US!

Necessity 8

Humanity

"The sole meaning of life is to serve Humanity."

- Leo Tolstoy

As an artist I always believed in the true theory of colours, we say that black exist because of white, light exist because of dark, depth and highlights both are contrasting off course, but both doesn't have existence without each other. It's up to us actually what we are looking for, if we are looking for darkness then there is a sure darkness. But what if we are in a very dark room, is it something that we won't be able to find lightness? We always look for lightness. Weird truth is most people doesn't look for lightness, they have grinded themselves too much in the darkness that they don't want to find the light.

Talking with people is as similar as this only, you have to keep on trying for the light, all you have to do is, you have to avoid all the darkness, and keep on looking for lights, you may have to face tons of darkness to find a little seed like lightness, but once you get to know the power of that small seed like lightness, you will know the tremendous possibilities of greatness the lightness can do. So whenever

I talk to anyone, I always try to search for that light. Let’s get through a powerful example.

What could be the possible desire for a person at the age of 20 23 may have, have you ever thought about it? Once I get to visit my elder brothers office, there is a person who was working over as an office boy, his main work was to open the office, close it, to do the cleaning work, to give coffee to everybody, to make tea for everyone, a little shopping work of outside, and these all are the work he used to do over there. His name is Vishal, he was swimming in between 20 to 23 years in age, when I get to my brother's office there was a kind of inauguration function was happening, and he was busy in taking care of all the things and duties over there. Wearing a brown colored jacket, an old shirt, a formal pant, and glossy shining black shoes, his hairs were oiled properly, properly combed, and above this all he was working very happily, when the function got over he got to me and asked

"bhaiya, would you like a coffee or a soup or something?"

Bhaiya is award over here usually used in place of Big brother. So when he asked me that I smiled on him, and I asked in return

"What's your name friend?"

He said

"My name is Vishal, bhaiya"

Then I said

"So Vishal bhai (Brother), I would love to have a coffee but there is a condition you have to give me company for that"

He smiled too and said

"Okay bhaiya, I am getting back to you with coffee"

after a while when he got back to me, he didn't get back with two cups, he was feeling a little shy and was not considering me and him good enough to take coffee together. So I said again to him

"Vishal I want to have coffee with you, can you please bring one more cup of coffee?"

He didn't say much and said

"Okay bhaiya I am coming"

"We think too much and feel too little. More than machinery, we need humanity. More than cleverness, we need kindness and gentleness."

- Charlie Chaplin

When he get back to me, I initially thought that this kid is working for money over here, and he is making his living, but the thing which attracted me to talk to him was his happiness while he was working, so I asked him

"What do you do over here Vishal?"

And he replied with a very mechanical answer as this answer was something he has mugged up, and he started something as an essay on what he do

"Bhaiya, almost all of the office works, I do dusting, I mob the floor, serve the coffee or tea to whole staff, if I have to get something from outside as shopping I do that too, and if somebody needs anything they ask me to do, and I take care of whole of the office"

When I heard this mechanical answer as it this question has been asked multiple times to him and this answer has been given so many times, of course he was considering me as younger brother of his boss, and I was willing to know and was wanting to dig him inside, to get the inspiration of him that how happy he is while working, you know it is a rare thing to find and most of the people around us, especially in those who are working for money.

So I asked him to make him a little comfortable

"Vishal bhai, don't you have a nickname or something?"

Now here, what came out, was not the mechanical answer, he answered me "my loved ones around me calls me Chotu"

Now the environment was a little comfortable.

Then I asked directly

"How is your family doing, chotu? How many siblings you have got? Tell me a little more about you chotu" now this Chhotu didn't hear these things often, and so he was not prepared for this question, although initially he was answering my questions as if I am interviewing him or interrogating him for something, with a confused look initially and then with the comfortable language

"He said my family is doing well, we are three brothers, I am the younger most, my elder most brother works in a medical company, and younger brother than him is jobless right now, and looking for a job around"

With these lines, I felt like to get to know his purpose and the reason of his wonderful attitude of working with this happiness is not going to be easy, a hard nut to crack.

The story got interesting from here, then I asked one more question, after which I did complete the digging in him, and found the gold, I asked

"Chotu, suppose, you have got three wishes, what will be the wishes you may ask, to fulfil?"

Well now he thought about it for a while, he was having a smile on his face, as if he never thought about it, or he often thought about the wish, but he was imagining it, as if the wish is already true now, and said with a smile

"I want to have dinner with the whole family"

That was not that shocking initially, thought like he gave it a second thought, could be faking, so I asked him again

"Chotu, do you go to your home late? Or do you live a little out of Indore city? I mean this is so obvious, you leave this office earlier, so you are able to have dinner daily with your family, why is it a wish",

Now this reply was touchy, he said

"No Bhaiya, I can't have dinner with my whole family, I had one dinner a year back, around March, and from that day I couldn't"

This was strange, I asked

"Why?"

Then he continued,

"I lost my father last year's march, I wanted to have dinner with him, that's my only wish, I don't want anything else"

"Love is the only way to rescue humanity from all ills."

- Leo Tolstoy

Now this statement somehow proved the first statement as a big truth, also proved that I was thinking a little weird about him, but now as the dams were open, he continued by himself

"Last year during March I came to visit my papa (Father) that was the last day I had dinner with him, the next day he was not with me to take dinner".

I again asked

"What happened there, if you are comfortable enough to tell?"

He said

"Papa was having some asthmatic issues already, I talked to him, and after an hour I went back to him, and he was no more, got an attack, and couldn't survive that, So I really miss him, after that day, my brothers and my family they all fight a lot altogether, my second wish will be only that I want them all to live happily,"

I asked what could be possible wish you could else ask for

"He said I don't need anything else sir, I have got everything else then this, next month I am going to vaishno maata mandir (A holy temple), I am already happy, boss has allowed me to go there too, he is a generous boss I have ever met"

I didn't have to ask much from him. I have found the lightness in him. And through this too, I can say he is a pure soul for sure.

Even after that meeting I started calling him Chotu, not vishal. Later that day, I asked my father who also joined my brother as an advocate, Advocate Shankar Lal Sir, after retirement, so he used to work with my brother Advocate Gagan Sir, and Vishal in the same office, the same thing about vishal. I asked

"Papa, if I would ask you that how is vishal as a person?"

He replied with the same thought and lightness I found

"He is a very honest and hardworking of a person, working with me for like 7 months, has got all the keys, he has got almost everything which may need security, but he already is too innocent to understand that, as he is a kid at the age of 21, just like, how we used to be, but honest enough to gain the trust of whole of the staff on him. A rare gem to find"

So the lightness in that honest boy, was shining, brother said he is a rare gem to find.

He was gem mainly because of the honesty, not because of educational qualifications he had right? And this is something which is not being taught in schools anymore. Off course there are stories they teach kids what promotes education. But I can ask you this, can a seed grow on a concrete road? NOO!

The concrete road may look beautiful, as beautiful as modern day's school, but if the school doesn't have values, it is as a big beautiful waste. If the sales people front desk are not honest, if the admission staff is not honest, and if the principal is not honest, and if the teacher is not having even an honest smile. How can they teach honesty to the souls of kid? It is again like something to pass on.

As I can't give you something I don't have, as I usually say, suppose if I need 5000 bucks in cash, the only person who can give me that cash is the person who has it, similarly if the person himself is not having honesty in him, how will he be able to give that to someone else, or a teacher can't pass on honesty if they don't have it. In a similar way a kid can never be honest through a teacher who is lying to parents about their kid, about his projects, this is not going to grow good.

"If it is not right do not do it; if it is not true do not say it."

- Marcus Aurelius

Isn't it true that love is the most required thing in the world for us? But often people consider humanity as love and care for human. But when I said humanity, then I meant a little more than that.

That was 1st of April 2024 I got a chance to witness a deed of a powerful soul with a very big heart. Although I was not knowing about it at the very first glance. I have got this habit of taking a tea usually in the evening at some tea shop.

When I was having one I saw a dog, who was seeming as if a street dog moving his tail in love, with two girls were walking towards him, they set at a place nearby with street dog they were calling Milky, and the dog was answering to that name, as he was theirs own, Milky was so much into them was so happy from the moment those two girls came over there, the moment was pretty eye catching.

The two girls were wearing some simple casual top and jeans must be under 25 in age. I initially thought this white dirty street dog could be their pet.

They set at a place nearby me, they were having a kind of big bag, in which they were having food was enough for not just one dog but many. Now, that was curious. Both girls were not into makeup, open hair wearing specs, and another one was simpler. I was curious enough and couldn't resist just to ask,

“Is he your pet?”

The moment I said so both of them were looking at each other as if they were asking the same question with each other. That was weirder, and they replied in a contrasting way one said

“Yes”

The other said

“No”

Then both said

“We just love him”

Their confusion was saying as if they have got a lot inside already. I continued
I have seen you often coming over here. Do you come here to feed him?”

That day both of the young girls drained a misunderstanding of mine that I am responsible person as per my age.

What I came to know was, one of the girls said,

"He is one of our favourites!"

"One of?"

I asked, and she said

"We meet 15 to 20 dogs a day, and he is one of our favourites"

Now, that felt, even after getting home, I kept thinking, that those two young girls were feeding more than 15 to 20 dogs everyday around them. I felt like this was something which is very rare to find and that was really impressive. Both of the girls were wearing casual clothes, they were earning a reasonable amount of money through a job each had. Most of us take responsibility for one, two or three people with us. And we feel like it's too much responsibility. And those two small shoulders were taking comparatively bigger responsibilities on them.

Later on, after a couple of days I had another encounter with them, they both were still feeding the same dog as I was in the same tea place. A lot can happen over tea, we were having tea with a group. The same dog was too much into them, so eager and so happy to be with them, he was not even letting them talk to us as like child as they often behave like. I could hit somebody with the speed of his tail, he was moving it. That was Lovely. That bonding in between them was overwhelming, I asked

“Do you just bring food for them? Just feed them? Or taking care of them too? Because this dog seems way near to you is behaving as you mean a lot to him”

She told me that

“We just do what the best possible we can”

Then I said

“He is behaving as if he just want to play with you a lot and stay in your arms only”

She replied

“I am just glad he is doing okay now”.

Now I was more curious and asked

“NOW?”

The reply was unexpected she said,

“Actually, he had a tumour, and he was so ill”

I asked,

“Are you doctor too, or something how did you come to know”

They were laughing a little and said

“No, I am just an artist, I know because we were there when he was getting operated”
Now this was touching as well as the curiosity increased more but before asking somehow she read my face and said

“We came to know that he is in some pain, we got him to a doctor, where he diagnosed him and said, He has got a tumour, and we have to operate him to make him fit again, we were trying to get him operated, as the doctor suggested”

Now I was wondering a lot and I asked out of curiosity

“Do you take care of their health as well like hospitals?”

She replied

“This time we didn't, I tried to do so, but the cost of operation was too high for us, so we had to take help from couple of NGOs, which we won’t ever want to take again”

That was overwhelming,

I asked

“You don’t want to take help from them? Even I was going to suggest that you would work with NGO’s, that way you will be able to do more of good around you, or may be, you will be able to take care of more dogs around you may be?”

What she said then is something heart crashing,

“Sir, finding a diamond out of stones isn’t that easy, and it is same with NGO’s, finding some good NGO, which actually wants to do something good for actual society or social work, is not easy.”

With a little shock I said,

“WHAT! They doesn’t’ help dogs or social works? ”

They replied one by one.

“Almost all the NGO’s are working for money, taking care of social works and society is something they have made business too, when we were trying to find something good for this milky, we found many.”

“And even couple of them were asking money from us, by saying their doctors are more capable and the expense of doctor is twice as more than this one.”

That wasn’t sounding good, I asked

“Still princess there has to be many expenses other than this getting to doctor diagnosing the disease seems like you are one of the rich one, born with a golden spoon”

Both were laughing a little and said

“This seems like a compliment to us, we both belong to a middle class family, trying to earn living through jobs”

I was like still? And she continued

"Almost half of our salary is usually consumed into these poor homeless cute happy creatures"

The moment I came to know that they are spending almost half of their salary on these dogs. And the way they were doing this activity that was amazing the feeling was extremely positive and I was so impressed. I am taking care of my family and other than that of course I am trying to do something good for the society but this gets in a kind of different powerful and appreciable approach towards making the whole place a better one to live.

Don't you think earning to make a living for us our self and our family, but considering the whole world a family is like almost a different dimension?

The point here I am trying to make is I may have to use some Hindi words over here I heard about these three words in Bhagavad Gita a holy book of ours. The one is Moh, second one is Prem, and the third one is Karuna. How they have described these three words with an example of considering oneself of father Dronacharya. Dronacharya was father of son named Ashwathama and he was so much into the love and care of his own son that is son got spoiled through that. I am not saying to get into that story but the God Vasudev Krishna over there in Bhagavad Gita was trying to explain Dronacharya that you have done some very bad deed for your son and what you are considering love for your son is something you didn't do anything for him. You did not do any good for your son.

The moment Dronacharya heard that he was so much confused and was like I did a lot for my own son why this Vasudev Krishna is saying like this. I love my son. At this moment Krishna explained those three words with the definition of love as Moh says I will give every possible happiness in the world to my son, this could be a good feeling but then son can get into bad company or the situation may get worse. With the second world Prem he explained that Prem says I will meet my son sufficient capable so that he will get and deserve all the possible happiness in the world. Prem is something which cares so much of his son. And there is this third term which is above love that is Prem, and Moh as well. That word is Karuna, Karuna is a spiritual and an God like quality God could be a small word over here, Karuna is something a quality of almighty Karuna means the love for each and every being, the same love a person may have for his own son or daughter the same love for each and every creature of the world this quality is basically Karuna.

Those two girls were the soul who are having this almighty like quality loving each and every one this is something one of the rare most quality possible.

If a person is rich people may say that he is able to feed or he is able to do good of more than 2000 people a day or a 5000 people, this could go for almost lakhs of people maybe. But let me ask you this is that rich person is spending half of his monthly effort comes into that as income or anything else? The answer is no he has got plenty, almost most of the rich people only spends a little of what they have and do the wonder through it according to them. But from my perspective spending almost half of what they are working hard for it is as similar as that they are actually working for the poor souls or we can say they are actually working for the love and care of their surroundings this than amazing feeling and this is something which is highly appreciable, act is not something that can always be supported it has got rules and regulations some philosophy is also there whether his or her doing is right or wrong what could be the possible effect of their doing. So I am not saying anything about that keeping their action aside, which are also good from my perspective too, but what is more important for me is, try to feel the intentions of them what they do and what they are doing is one of the best deed I have ever seen in my entire life, especially at this age whatever they are doing is from their own wisdom what so ever they have. But from my perspective this is amazing.

This is something I believe we should have, or at the minimum the education must have, or we can deliver the same to our loved ones, why it is important. This single thought that we are ruling the planet is way dangerous thought. This thought is damaging the whole ecosystem putting us on the top of everything, which is not just weird bad too.

Suppose for once, we are not humans we are rose plants, and rose plants are us. If they cut our kids as flowers roses, and sell our kids for their pleasure? Or if we were chickens instead of humans, and they could be us, the chickens were keeping us all day awake and make us eat only and not just that put us in a single cage all without any clothes with so many above us one by one waiting for death, to cut and to become their food once. God has given us power to become human there are plenty of examples and lives 87 lakhs of species are there, only the human doesn't respect life.

If we consider any of the holy book in the world, if almighty has created all the creatures as his own sons and daughts, than every creature is our brother, think like this we are not just eating them which is somehow part of ecosystem, even a lion eats other animals, a cow eats grass, but it's a part of ecosystem they don't do them for fun. You may never see a cow saying to another cow lets collect grasses for fun, let's see who can collect more. They only fulfil their stomach energy needs and no creature ever disturbs life, they all respects life except one creature. Why am I saying this?

Take an example of one big family, there is one father, one mother, 2 sons, once a son believed that if I will give my father some offerings or my mother some offerings then they might be happier. If one son cuts the fingers of other son, and puts it on a plate and offer to the father and prays my father, please bless me with happiness? You tell me by yourself will father bless him with happiness or going to be angry on him?

In a very similar way, offering flowers to any politician, or gods, or almighties on the name of offering or welcoming, is disrespecting life for entertainment or for the name of respect for humans, they are also our siblings from the ultimate power or almighty whatsoever name you can give to them.

It's not just true with some things, we are believing we are ruling the world and do some disgusting tasks too from my perspective, suppose if one person murders another one for any reason it's a crime. We say that you can't take life of another, but if the same person is taking life of another ones, say a bridge is being made plenty of plants have to die, if a township is to be made, thousands of animals birds, insects have to leave their shelter and so may have to die too. Just because we call if growth, can't their be a middle way. Take an example of bridges, we can replant those 100's of years old trees somewhere else too. But that would be expensive so we focus on pieces of paper which government calls currencies which is somehow made by those trees only. And these all crimes are not even crimes in laws. 1000's of liters milk is waster on the name of offerings to almighty, cloths on the name of almighty, so many flower plants has to die on the name of almighty, so many things are used from us on the name of almighty, which are life in itself, who feels pain just like us when they are cut, and we give them pain on the name of offering and believes almighty is going to bless us, trust me this way almighty may be angry on you, but happy, ummm NO CHANCE!, in face get ready for punishment.

"God gives us things to share, God doesn't give us things to hold."

- Anonymous

Anyways about our main motive here, let's get to a solution based approach here. In our world if any accident happens over a road, most of the time people what look for is, how much loss my vehicle has got? Not how much loss the person or any other life has affected by this. And this is what my main concern here is. We should love people, and use things. Not just people, as I have mentioned above as well a god like quality is Karuna, if we can possess that quality or if we can teach that quality to our kids that would be really amazing.

Respecting life is something can give us what they and we actually deserve, we get apples, food from different things for our survival for our life, it's time to show our gratitude back to mother earth. What happens in almost all of the schools is, prayers are there talking about the good things, showing gratitude towards almighty towards mother earth, but truthfully how many students actually know or understand the true meaning of it? I appreciate the work, but I really believe if the school isn't able to do that we should try to teach our kids our loved ones about how much thankful we should be. We want best for our kids, and that's the reason we always try to tell them this is good this is bad, this is where you should be more careful and this is where you should be aware of situations. Whatever we do is something what we have got from our experiences good or bad. But let me ask you this, are our experiences same as our parents? Or anyone in our family? Isn't everyone is unique and explores a whole new world through his own eyes?

So talking about or teaching about this is how you should behave to bad or good, isn't it something that we should let them explore. Off course we should hold their back, but letting them explore their own world through their own eyes, teaching them and making the quality of Karuna is going to be more precious and will be very much helpful for their whole life. When they would feel love and will respect life and others, this is the only way they will be more kind. Don't we want our loved ones to be kind? We should begin this from ourselves off course. The way we can make everyone around us kinder. Off course it is already there in most of the kids' school syllabus, as Moral science. But I would actually want them to understand it not for good marks, but to be a better of a person.

"Kindness is the best for of humanity."

- Doris Lee

Ending this on a good note, I remember those words,

"If you are kind, people may accuse you of selfish,

Interior motives.

BE KIND ANYWAY.

What you spend years building, someone could

Destroy overnight.

BUILD ANYWAY.

The good you do today, people will often

Forget tomorrow.

DO GOOD ANYWAY.

Give the world the best you have, and it may

Never be enough.

GIVE THE WORLD THE BEST YOU'VE

GOT ANYWAY.

You see, in the final analysis, it

Is between you and your God....

ANYWAY."

On the wall of an orphanage in Calcutta, India.

So may the ripple of this goodness continue to the end of the world and spread as air. Be the best of you always, and anyways.

Necessity 9

Survival

"Survival is the ability to swim in strange water."

\- Frank Herbert

Let's be honest, from the day we get life, we get comfortable with the environment with time, but very first time isn't always necessarily pleasing, the moment we leave our mother's body, we start to cry first. Doctor even considers that the cry is important, that cry isn't a sign of bad thing, but our uncomfortability, than we get close to our mother again, and with time we get comfortable with our environment.

Almost similar situation is with almost every relation we have, he is grandfather, grandmother, brothers, sisters, everyone around us, we first have the introduction as a stranger may be through feeling or may be through language we get comfortable with them.

Similarly the schooling the first day, we get close to the people we are unfamiliar with, then we make friends, we make an image of a teacher then we get comfortable there. Parents are almost always with us to face every unfamiliar situation. But truthfully we have to be someone where we could manage the strange and unfamiliar environment familiar by ourselves.

We should actually be trained for the unknown, we should be prepared for the unknown. And getting through what life throws at us is basically called survival.

"Success is survival."

Leonard Cohen

Once I was with my friends and we were going for a dinner. A kid could be around 10 or 12 years in age he came to me and the he was asking overall for money. He was a beggar, he was wearing that green old teared apart sweater and an old dirty grey pant as if it has been given from somebody else as those clothes were not of his size. Dust can easily be seen on his face and on his hair a little oily and dusty as if he didn't take bath as well from days. He was having a photo of a holy God in India we say Mata Lakshmi. And in the same bucket there was a red cloth and the picture of holy God was there. He came to me and bagged for money using couple of words in Hindi. He said

"Bhaiya Daya karke kuchh rupaye de do Mata ji aapka khyal rakhenge"

If I'll be using or translating these words in English then I would be saying that he was asking for money and he was over all saying that if he will give me money then the god will have mercy on me. When he said to me that I was on my cell phone I stopped for a while. I looked that kid and I asked him

"What is your name son?"

He said

"Shailendra".

When he said his name his name was he said in Hindi but I will try to say the same words are similar words in English for better understanding as well. I said to Shailendra

“My son I will give you money if you could please tell me the meaning of word you used that is 'dayaa'."

The moment I asked him with love he had a kind of smile on his face. He smiled at me and said very cutely

"I don't know".

I and my friends found this curtness very cute we laughed a little on it, after couple of seconds I asked Shailendra again

"My son, if you don't know the meaning of this, then why are you using these words?"

He replied to me

"Because I want money".

Then I asked him

"How old are you Shailendra?"

He answered me

"I am 8 years old"

His age was clearly visible on his face, and with this question with him I came to know couple of things that whatever he is talking about he is trained well, when I felt as if he is trained, how much training and 8 year young can get? So I decided to give him a deal just so I could teach him something good that could help him. I said to him

"My son, let me buy you food"

My intentions were to make his stomach full he should not feel hungry. He said

"My stomach is full I just need money, not food".

I was confused a little, he just 8 years young and he is desperately looking for money, so I thought what else 8 year young could ask for, what he may do with money?, so I started giving him couple of options

"My son do you want to buy a chocolate, some clothes, any food, or anything I can buy for you?"

He was not moving forward with the discussion he was stuck at only one place. He said

"I want money, will you be kind enough to give me money, and god will have mercy upon you."

I really felt weird, and I couldn't stop myself to ask him

“My son, if you do not want me to buy any of these what else will you do with money?"

And he said

"I'll be buying food for my family."

Then I said

"Can I buy food for your family? How many members are there in your family?"

He said

"There are seven members in my family, including four siblings of mine"

I said

"Okay Shailendra let's go and buy food for your family"

Shailendra stopped me again and said

"I do not need cooked food, please give me packaged raw food, we will be cooking by our self"

I thought this is making more of a sense maybe and said

"Okay Shailendra we can do that, there is a mall near by.... "

My friend stopped me there and my friend was saying, that

"Rahul I believe you should give him something which is not packaged, it should be open"

I was wondering why he may have said that and asked the same

"What difference does it gone going to make friend",

My friend was having a weird smile and he said.

"If the person is not having place to live, they do not have food to eat, then how come they may have kitchen or related articles?, our friend Shailendra is going to sale those products which is going to get from you, on more of a reasonable price then what you will be paying"

My friend was also making sense but this was not that so much trust worthy, so I made another choice to talk with Shailendra again and asked him

"Shailendra will it do if I would give you something which is not packaged food, something raw".

The moment Shailendra heard this he was saying

"No I do not want that."

I didn't like that answer so I asked him, do you have home"

He said

"No I do not have",

Then I asked

"Do you have kitchen at your place?"

He again said

"No I do not have".

Then I asked

"Then you must have something to cook, gas or something, how are you going to cook food through that raw material".

Now he was silent a little. I was having one chocolate in my pocket I offered him and said

"My son, I want to help you, and if you would be honest with me I will be able to help you more, now please take chocolate and tell me the truth"

All the time he was having that kind of serious face that as if he is in trouble, after seeing the chocolate, he was having a little smile on his face, and then he said

"I am supposed to give that packaged food to my uncle, and he will give me money through that"

Now that was a little shocking then I asked him

"Where do you live son?"

He said

"I live near by the Next Street",

Then I ask him

"What do you do with this money? Then?"

And he give me an honest answer

"This is my work and this is what I have to do."

I said again

"Don't you feel like you should be studying?"

He said

"I don't know, why to study, every educated person here around is giving me money what they are earning, it is their work and this is my work, I spend my whole day over here I can eat whatever I want, I can go whenever I want, and wherever I want, I don't have to ask for any permission from anyone, I am free, and everybody here around is educated like you, when I hear them they always complain about freedom, they don't have leaves, they don't have time, they don't have money too, they always say, I can't afford eating this often, they can't but I can, they want this they want that, I mean I am a kid, I don't know why to study, and if this is something that could make me clean, and sad, so I am okay here."

His line was sounding dangerous there, "they can't, but I can!" Definitely put me in thought, but I had one more point there, I said to him that day,

"My son if you will be studying enough you will be a better person and then you can give money to somebody who is in need like you."

He said

"Are you serious? I am 8 years and age of this is what I am doing, I am working I am going to give money to my siblings and my friends just like you do"

"The best view comes after the hardest climb."

- Benjamin Franklin

You know one weird thing, that time I was stunned for a moment, he was at the end of finishing is chocolate, and I was in the beginning of thinking, that I get to see my siblings once or twice a year, and in the same way, he is doing better than me, I thought a little, stopped myself for a while, and asked the kid,

"Kid do you want to go to an orphanage or something, I can get you there."

He said

"I have been there, I don't want to go there, I am happy here, and if you could please buy me some packaged food so that I could get that to my home"

I smiled a little, all of my friends were smiling, and Shailendra started to smile too, I asked him

"Other than this, can I drop you at your home Shailendra?"

He said

"No that's okay I will go after an hour or two"

I said

"How will you go than?"

He said

"I'll be going by bus. Or maybe somebody will drop me there"

Now, Shailendra was very much comfortable with me, a kind of friend, and the thought what I had in mind that I should not be giving him money I should be buying him something as food or something to full fill his stomach, was all wasted, and I gave up on him, cause in some sense he was making sense, of course not completely but in some sense we all were not making much sense, so at last I said

"Can I buy you bus ticket?"

Now Shailendra was having a little smile on his face and the naughty attitude, his clothes were dirty, he didn't take bath from days, he was looking all dirty, I still remember his face and with that cute smile, he was very much content, that contentment which I have seen that day in him was something that I notice very rarely. So with the same naughty attitude, he said

"I have got money, thank you for the chocolate."

"People raised on love see things differently than those raised on survival."

- Joy Marino

Now I was like all blank, and speechless, Shailendra vas going away from me, and I really wanted to do something for him, I was not at all feeling content, I was initially feeling bad for him when I started talking with him, but now I was not feeling that so much good for me neither for my friends, so I shouted his name one more time when he was a little away "SHAILENDRA!" And what he did was, he only gave me a look, and winked on my face.

He definitely may be wrong somewhere, I am not supporting begging, but there are so many questions which arise through this incident, and I still wonder at his question. "Why to study?"

"To ask the right questions is already half the solution of a problem."

- Carl Jung

Let me ask you this, in our life we always tend to plan something, and we always expect our plan to workout. How often whatever we plan is something that happens exactly the way how we planned it? Well you and I both know the answer of this question not very often.

This mean that there is something which is going to happen which is not in our plan, and if something happens which is not our plan is something which has happened unexpected. Whenever something unexpected happened to us, the reaction to that situation is not always good actually that reaction is something which makes our life miserable. Most of the people in the world are not able to take care of an unexpected situation or an unexpected event.

Life is full of unexpected things so don't you think that we all should be more prepared for something that is unexpected and that is one thing that proves the requirement to learn the survival skills.

This unexpected definitely includes something very good or something worst. If we are ready for something then definitely we can do better at that situation. As an example suppose we are well prepared for an expected event consider an example of interview. When we are expecting the event of an interview to happen we will definitely work on our self to prepare that. And if our preparation will be good enough then I am pretty sure we tend to be happy at that situation, and handles that interview and comparatively way better way.
But if something really bad happens to us and if we are not prepared for that we are going to handle that situation in one of the bad most possible way. This is one of the requirement from my perspective that we should be ready for everything.

I have got a sister of mine in Canada the temperature over there is very low. The kind of temperature India is never going to face, at least In the city I live. That was the time of January and December I was talking to her and her kids were also playing in the background. 4 years ago as she was from India and she used to live with us the language comparison was very convenient she was able to communicate very properly in Hindi and she was able to communicate in English as well. After 4 years her kid's one son of something 8 years in age and a daughter at 12 years of age both were talking to me in English language only even their accent has changed completely.

I was talking to them and my sister said

"Brother the temperature over here is too low, once I went to pick my kids at school, I was initially thinking that how my kids are going to survive in this climate, but they have done it pretty well better than me, it is all snow all around here once I saw them playing outside of the school the temperature was something minus 6 degrees over here and my son took a ball of snow from the ground, and was taking it as if it is an ice cream, and they were playing with it pretty well. They just got out of their gym class."

I stopped her at that very moment and asked

"Did you say gym class?"

And she replied

"Yes brother we have got a compulsory gym classes in the school syllabus, and my kids are attending gym classes in school regularly as a physical activity, here at my place they focus on survival skills in prior to technical knowledge, the education system over here is more towards practical skills which are going to help them in their survival at the later age"

I said

"Sister I agree about the survival is necessary to teach but what is the hurry over there?"

And what she said is

"Here they are not just serious about survival skills they work a lot for that, everybody's mindset here is in the same kind of situation, if a child works in his childhood then only he gets his pocket money"

I asked her with a confusion

"If a child work, child labor is prohibited right?"

She laughed and said

"Brother you are taking it in a wrong direction, by work I mean they teach children to do their own work like take care of their clothes, they have to take care of their bed, basic works a children should know for his own sake, if there taking care of them then only they gets pocket money, as the soon have to find their own home"

As I was in India this statement was a little confusing again,

"What do you mean by his own home? He has got parents right what is the need of it if he is living with the parents?"

I asked.

She answered me again with the smile

"Brother we here have got a world of difference in cultures over here in comparison with India, at the age of 18 something almost every kid here leaves their parents' home, and he has to find his own shelter to live and start his own journey, when the sun or daughter gets to the age of 18 even parents starts saying so that he should be on his own now then only heel be able to learn the actual survival, definitely does not mean leaving the parents actually, but they are going to meet on festivals and such, but this is there way of teaching survival and independency."

"I'm a fighter. I'm a survivor, and I'll get through anything people can throw at me."

- John Daly

You know india was also having a kind of similar environment initially when all this education system was created, I am not talking about the era right now we are into I am talking about the place where the ancient culture was there, where there used to be Gurukuls, in India a child was to go to a Gurukul at the young age of something 4 5 6 years and they gets back to home after their complete education tell the age of 18 years just so they can understand the independency the survival skills and of course the Gurukul was having so much related education system syllabus over there. Of course there were so many works to do by students to even manage the Gurukul some used to do cleaning, some were assigned to do Dusting, somewhere assigned to collect food, some for the help in cooking, with plenty of physical activities in prior, education for science physics chemistry math's, and such other things. The syllabus had everything for a child to understand the actual survival in priority. Of course in Gurukuls a child has to leave the home a way little earlier, but the purpose here of both of the education system is same, and at the least the intentions are very pure of teaching the kid about the survival and making them mentally and physically fit. The education was more into creating wisdom in the mind of a child. Don't you think wisdom is much more required then education?

Although almost so many of us feels a little shame at saying something what they may have done in the form of struggle or at the beginning of their success journey, which I believe it should be shared with everyone, atleast a good example has to be set, we all have done something good or bad things to be successful or to be what we are right now, I believe this should be told to our loved ones at the minimum, with do's and don'ts, so that they could understand, what should be done, and what shouldn't be done too.

Through this only, we will be able to build some powerful wisdom in our kids to understand what is justifiable for our survival and what shouldn't be done at any cost. So that the cost of success will always be bearable. Whatever we have done to be successful has made us strong. I remember one line which would definitely be helpful as.

"Survival is your strength not your shame."

- T. S. Eliot

Though matter is not just the shame, as I mentioned previously, almighty the supreme power has not made an discrimination between any have you ever seen a person getting out of an expensive comparing works as small or big by ourselves is not an appreciable thing, Is some work is small or some are big? There is no discrimination in between any of the life forms from the perspective of almighty or almost any other creature in the world, the only creature who believe they are superior than the other is human. This superiority feeling has already made a lot of damage to the world too, No other creature believes that they are superior than us, now because of this feeling of superiority, we do the same thing with other humans too, black or white, rich or poor, we even make the people discrimination through their work too, he do dusting, he mobs the floor so he is small person, he operates a factory so he is a small person. Let me ask you this, does the person getting out of a branded car, if you will observe closely they don't get out of the car walking with their hand, even I have observed them by myself too, that they had two eyes just like us, they have got two hands just like us, they actually are just like us, I did the same for bagger, we are exactly alike, then what could be the possible reason for this discrimination?

In actual this feeling of being superior is making this issue, and this is the topmost issue in killing the happiness of someone, even there are so many laws there too, that it is illegal to discriminate on any basis, the reason I was wanting this to be discussed here is, if you ever observe a tree or plant, even if all the roots are cut, it again begins from the beginning and starts to grow from the very basic plants, because this is what they do, the basic nature in every being is survival, and they all do that happily and daily.

We do that too, but this discrimination especially through work is my focus here, as we have discussed the comparison topic previously too. But how is this related here?

"Discrimination is not done by villains. It's done by us."

- Vivienne Ming

Once I got a chance to meet an IT expert. Let's try to make this more interesting, through another story through his perspective too.

Just like almost everybody I was having kind of expectations that after completing my education I would have a good job and in school books, they tried trying feature everything except how to get a job. I have read so many books other than school too so that I could find one because my parents think through education my son will be able to earn money, so even I thought the same, that in education I will be able to learn how to earn money, but my expectations and reality was not matching. They are telling us about the geographical condition of the world, political condition, moral values, science, mathematics, what we should do, what we should not, but how to earn money is available nowhere.

This is the exact place where one can get easily confused, I mean if books do not have answers then maybe people do. Suddenly I saw an advertisement "Are you looking for a job??" I said yes yes I am looking for that, "are you tired of finding the answer of question how to get a good job?" This YouTube advertisement was something I didn't skip, and maybe this YouTube person somehow knows what I am looking for, anyways I kept watching the ad as I was feeling like, "How did he come to know that I am looking for a good job". So I said, full of excitement, "yes yes I am looking for a job, of course, a good job"

There are found their contact details, and I got their address, full of excitement, I started my bike to the final destination of my dream job, I couldn't stop smiling, as the feeling of finding a good job, is like a dream come true.

"Mam, I saw your advertisement, and I need a job, please tell me what I have to do?"

Mam's reply was a little obvious, but still promising.

"Please fill this form, with your contact details"

I filled that form in a couple of minutes and felt like I was the fastest man alive. After reading the form, they said.

"You have got good qualifications, we are pretty sure we can get your job."

They had confidence, and I had sparkles in my eyes, even I was imagining my new iPhone I was going to buy, and the bike, suddenly my ears got straightened a noise came,

"You just have to pay half of your salary"

All the dreams went in vain. Woke up after the completion of the sentence they said

"Of the first month, we mean" that was expensive too, but the job is more important. So let's focus I said yes.

Previously I used to see the phone every minute for my friends, especially the girl I meant. But then I used to see my phone for the call from this consultancy and trust me not for romantic reasons, although the receptionist was beautiful, but dreams, career, and job are important. I just received the call from them, very excited now.

"Yes Mayoor, you have got an interview, tomorrow"

I got so excited,

"Okay mam, I will be there where it is?"

They replied with similar excitement

"Vijaynagar area, Jash technologies"

Suddenly my excitement fell to the ground, and I said

"Mam I don't think you will be able to get me a job now"

With a little confused voice, they said, a well mugged up line

"We have made more than 1800 placements so far in your industry, why do you think like this Mayoor?"

I said,

"Mam I have already been there almost a week ago, a friend of mine got me an interview there, and not just me everybody around me in my class has been there, Bad workplace, and after a wait of 15 days you got me this? Seriously?"

I really love this thing of salespeople they don't argue if they can lose sales, even with this disgusting feeling, they said

"We get you Mayoor, we will find something more suitable for you, give us one more chance to prove ourselves"

I have to say, This much confidence in speech is what I want, they got me excited again, and the dreams became a little smaller comparatively like a bike instead of a car now, Goa instead of Sydney, but still, I was dreaming. They seemed good people and 1800 plus placements are there I will be getting a good job.

I am an IT professional, technology is a piece of cake for me, and I love this technology so much. That's why I spend most of my time on Instagram. Don't judge me please, instagram is technology too. Saw a couple of reels on Instagram, that people are getting good packages through IT work, Some are saying that Patience is the key, Right door is just the next one, although I believe it's enough time I have spent being unemployed. I was chatting to a friend of mine at night. Poor people gave up on their wonderful IT careers. Now they are working as a CCE, at TP. This short form seems cuter but it is one of the lowermost salary jobs in town, made for anyone after 12th class, as a customer care executive. I am made for something big. A friend told me, but with something this big, I am not able to sleep properly, too much technology time, on social media, can take your sleep away. It’s almost 3 am now, I should be sleeping.

Phone rings. It's one of my favourite ringtones though, but it does not seem like a favourite for now. I am sleeping brother, and I have just got into bed. So I put the phone on vibration. It's not even 5 minutes I put it on vibration, and it started vibrating again, what the hell? I looked at it, Oh Myyy God, they are the consultancy people. Got excited and confused too. Why in hell they are calling at 5 in the morning? But I picked up, and thought they might be in some important things, but if they will be asking money at this time, I swear I will grab their neck at the office right now.

"Hello"

I was already sleepy, it’s 5 in the morning brother,

"haeeelloo"

"Hello Mayoor, We have got you an interview"

I lost the sleep in a second.

"Woww, when, in which company?"

Was that too much excitement? But they almost killed me by saying...

"In Jash Technologies"

That's a big name they said, I had some big stars in my eyes.

"Seriously? Ohhh thanks!"

But their next line got me stars on my head rolling.

"Get ready now, in just five minutes you will be having the best interview of your life."

Wait a minute, NOW? Now? I just slept, what kind of company takes the interview at morning 5 am? This is bad, and worst is I haven't got up, I needed to bath, shower, and get ready. How can they do this to me?

"What the hell are you talking about? How am I supposed to get ready in five minutes? Which company takes the interview at 5 in the morning?"

They were so calm.

"Mayoor, its 11 am, is your clock working properly?"

Shoot, I am writing shoot in English, said something else in Hindi though, but seriously, it was too late, suddenly I felt bad. My first best interview is in 5 minutes from now.

"Ooh, ssssorry mam, my bad, I was somewhere else, Let me, let me please get ready for an interview, where do I have to come?"

And she was still helping

"Nooo! Mayoor, You don't have to come anywhere, It will be an online interview, and you have to attend from there only, get a formal shirt, and get a computer, i will be sharing a Zoom meeting link, in a while, and Best Wishes!"

You know me right, the fastest man alive, at least right now, I rushed to the bathroom, washed my face, opened my computer, took the sexiest formal black shirt I had, and opened my WhatsApp on the computer, I am an IT expert you know. And then all set ready with my specs on. and I have to admit, the fastest man alive, wearing a White painted patterned, cool dude chadda, half pant below, and a formal shirt above, they are going to see the upper part of me right, and I was out of time too, I am again talking to you, the link is already there in the inbox. Shhh, let me focus on the interview now.

4 Beautiful faces were there on the computer, who were taking interviews, 2 male and 2 female, yes I am saying beautiful as the males were also well dressed, and all had big smiles on their faces, females were born beautiful of course. I was also having a smiling face. Got the first question hit from the male person. They gave me a code to solve it again.

What the hell! Seriously? I mean the technical round was already clear, I did answer those questions already, and they are asking me to do that again, I wasn't prepared for that, I was prepared for the Final interview now, salary has to be talked about, and we will be good to go. My ears were having some noises

"Mayoor? Mayoor, can you see the code?"

I said, with a very educated voice. You know calm and composed, at least I have to behave so.

"Yes sir, I can see that, sir"

"Can you solve it"

They asked, I did see the code, and I am an IT expert but the question was seeming as if it was not made for IT experts, how am I supposed to solve this, wait a minute I remember now.

"Yyyes sir, I can solve it"

I started solving it, my tongue was tolerating my teeth biting it, with thinking expressions as if I was writing, the constitution with the codes, and now they were disturbing me.

"Mayoor, are you solving the code now?"

"Yes, Yesss sir, I am solving it!"

My confidence is at its pinnacle. At the top,

"Did you share your screen? Somehow we are not able to see it?"

Oh my god, you idiot, I felt like an idiot brother, I am an IT expert you know it, and didn't share the screen, I saw the screen, and you know what, I used to think that a woman was the enemy of women, but now the men were laughing at me a little, And respect is above everything

"Ohhh, sorry sir, I forgot, 2 minutes please"

It's not like I can't talk much, but I was not able to. And Being an IT expert, it feels so bad to say, I wasn't an IT expert, the confidence was rolling down the hill now. Everyone was staring at me, I was able to see myself too at the screen, thank god I wear specs, and instead of my eyes they were able to see my glowing specs only.

"Are you having any trouble, Mayoor?"

What a beautiful voice there she had, woww, I fell for them. But with a very humiliated and almost negligible volume of voice, I said

"Mam, actually, I do not see the option to share the screen"

This fact was heart-breaking to accept, but I did, a strong non-IT expert. But that beautiful voice

"Let me guide you here, Can you see the three dots at the right upper corner of the screen, you will find that there"

Oooh myyy god. I have to say, how kind they were, how helpful they were, what the hell will I do with salary, consider me an orphan, and please take me home with you. I was literally thinking, I am lost, just take me, please. such good people, I can spend the rest of my life with you.

"Yes yes mam, that's so kind of you, thanks for the help, I can see that now"

They were still calm, so good of them brother, if I were one of them, I would have kicked myself out for sure.

"Now we can see your screen too Mayoor, please carry on, and complete the code"

I said "Yes mam, Let me please"

You know what, I really think I am no longer an IT expert, even if I shouldn't call myself one of them. I hate the fact, that I forgot the code I was writing. I was all blank and wasn't typing anything.

"Sir, I am not able to remember that now, I am sorry, I think I forgot"

I was already feeling sorry, and I wanted to be with them for sure. but not sure what else to do here. They were talking to themselves only.

"Do any of you want to ask anything to Mayoor?"

"No, No, I don't"

Such Harsh words, in a Kind tone through those beautiful people and 2 angels were coming out and a little relaxing line is what I got.

"Mayoor, we don't have any other questions for now, we will be notifying you, and you can leave the meeting now"

They will be notifying me, so kind people, they were still at least saying so. I courageously said the best possible words.

"Okay Mam, Thank you"

With a smile, I ended up the meeting,

Trust me I was all blank for a while, I wasn't able to talk, or do anything for a couple of minutes, then I came to know, that a more important thing was missing here, I was feeling hungry, I didn't eat anything since I was asleep.

Anyway, this was really heart-breaking. My confidence is something that was rolled almost down to my feet, my toe was touching it as if an ant was under it. I opened my Instagram again, reels were saying keep on trying, and I decided to do so,let's prepare better to be an IT expert originally. I will be reading 6 to 8 hours a day from today onwards. Now there was one more reel, saying we should be independent, I thought yes they are right too, till how long I will rely upon my parents, I should have a job by now. Then another reel came out, if you can't fly, run, if you can't run, walk, if you can't walk, crawl, but keep moving forward, no matter how small you begin. but move. I am convinced too, look I know customer care executives could be a bad idea, but we should be independent, we should not stop. And customer care executive is sounding bad, but CCE ummmm it doesn't. So I called my friend for a CCE post and got another interview.

I opened Instagram again, they were saying never to lose hope. Being an optimistic person. I am still waiting for their call. I have everything a good person should have. I will indeed have a great future ahead. The best a boy can get.

A story from Mayoor's perspective, Of course he is a happiness expert, and not an IT expert but the thing I was trying to learn from this is the person is happy enough until he was trying to do something that may be he wasn't mean to do, definitely I am not a judge here that who should decide whether he should be doing that or not but the thing here is from the birth his parents were so much concerned about his career and future. So they always use to teach him that you should study as we could not his father was farmer and mother was almost farmer and domestic engineer I should be saying. They know how to cook the food how to grow the food of best quality for us and for themselves, as well. But as they were focusing on him to be an educated person, which he was trying to be, they didn't let him understand the concepts of food cooking or growing.

"Whoever is happy will make others happy."

\- Anne Frank

Now, he is all grown up, still in the city, once I got to meet him again, I asked him

"How the life is here"

He was not fond of life here he said

"what to say bhaiya the life is almost help without my mother's food I really miss my place but I don't know what else to do my parents are wanting me to be here to be an IT expert and educated person they want me to do a job here which I don't want to do."

I asked

"Then, why do you miss your mama handmade food here"

He said

"The homemade food is of high quality and this outside food in city is beautiful but it is really bad for me, it is not affecting my health daily as I have to eat outside almost daily."

I asked

“Then why don't you cook by yourself as your mother was able to do you could do that to at least as it is affecting your survival.”

He said

“bhaiya I don't know how to cook food.”

I said

“Okay, then may be, you can try couple of cooking videos as well.”

He said
“yes bhaiya, I have tried that to food from my hand is almost taste like poison.”

I asked him again

“Then, how will you survive like this.”

His reply is still in my ears,

“I don't know bhaiya, I am doing a job for my survival, and maybe my job is my survival.”

This was really heart breaking for me, He was having so many weird marks on his face as if a kind of some skin allergy reaction is there. I asked him with curiosity

“You seem fit, physically strong as well then why are these spots are there on your face.”

He said with a sad face

"bhaiya, when I got to the city couple of my friends were going to gym fitness centre and to gain more of the muscles my gym trainer suggested me some powder based protein."

I said

"okay, that could be the reason of your physical fitness."

He said

"working out and going for a gym is something has made me fit for sure but, I am not sure about that protein after taking that for a week I started having the patches on my skin when I consulted a doctor and the doctor give me some treatment and told me that this protein was somehow the reason of this reaction and I have to stop taking it from now on, but till then I had so many dark spots on my face and body, that treatment doctor gave me was helpful a little, these patches got a little lighter but, it's been years now, I really don't think these purchase are going to get away now."

Well he took the protein without consulting a doctor and again the same thing the gym trainer was surviving on selling those protein powder which I am not sure about. Anyways a very pure soul I have met that day but wasn't comfortable in surviving through an IT expert wasn't table to survive through the food he was cooking he wasn't able to get to his hometown as the parent think that he should be an educated one but, now his father's farming skill is something he didn't get his mother's cooking skill is something he didn't get, he did get a meaning of surviving through struggle from the world that struggling in the city for some money is something what the survival is.

My question to you is this, what the survival means for today is? For educated people too, as an example

A survival skill for a painter has become painting

A survival skill for an engineer is engineering,

Survival skill for every professional person has become their profession and when the profession is something gets in trouble there survival automatically gets in trouble

Take an example of painting, initially the wall painters who used to paint advertises they used to get a lot of money which they used to call survival they used to hire so many juniors and were making a huge money.

After sometime flex printing machine came into existence and suddenly the job for printers become a very low paid job and the people who are not able to do anything else made the profession of painting as their survival their survival become typical. Similarly later on digital painting was there, canvas painting, Canvas printing was there,

There was a job of a cameraman and the helicopter and the person who used to fly the helicopter they all couldn't survive properly just because the Automatic drone has come into existence.

I am not against of technology you may find a quote that, the people who are not going to change won't be able to survive, I want you to take it in a different way, as I always say Android 2.0 has to be better than Android 1.0, right? Then only, we can call it growth or development. Same is true for ourselves as well, what kind of change is this, why can't we learn basic surviving skills like cooking food at least for ourselves, if we stuck somewhere we teach our kids independency then we ask our kids to depend on other technology or may be us.

"If you are not getting better, you're getting worse."

\- Draymond Green

Anyways this was a wonderful story said by Mayoor, one of the very kind and pure-hearted people I have ever met, But if I have to talk about my opinion too. The story should be helping, at the topic right?

- Do you know the number of educated people who are looking for a job, or so called their survival, is only similar to the population of Bengaluru?

- 82% of males and 92% of females earn less than 10,000 INR a month. Source azimpremjiuniversity.edu.in, Trust me surviving at this amount is way typical.

- Only 1.6% of the youth is able to earn more than 50,000INR a month.

Not just that, 7 out of 10 employees complain about the job. This mean that their survival process is something has become way complicated and a process of something they aren't loving, they are hating.

What I am trying to say is, on the basic education till 12th class, even if we consider the cost of education is 50000INR a year, it is something 8Lakhs for the education only for the child's development. After the 12th out of imagination expenses for education are there here in India people are paying more than crore to make their son and daughter be a doctor, MBBS. MBA students, MCA there are 100's degrees available. Even if I consider only 20lakh INR for upper education. They struggle for that and call it survival for them as well as for their loved ones.

Considering the kid has above average income of more than 10,000INR, say 20000INR is something he begins working with. Usually at the age of 23 to 25 maximum. It will take around 10 years minimum only to get the amount invested in his education. Only the education I am talking about, by this 10 years he will be 33 or 35 years of age. I am talking about an average educated person. The situation is already worse than this. What kind of survival this could possibly be?

Society doesn't stop here, they have a social trap too, marriage is here, a home has to be bought, and a car. His entire life is going to be utilized/used/wasted in these for sure. You can put any word here, out of these three.

Things won't stop here, he will be busy doing the same for his kids, the same education loans are there, and the same EMI's and Easy Monthly Instalments become, Easy Maaro Insaan, (Easy Kill Human). Trust me surviving through any of these isn't that easy at all.

> "The thing that gives you power also traps you."
>
> \- Eckhart Tolle

Is this something we all are preparing for as Survival?

Is this the life we actually are hoping for?

Will this be the life of a pure soul of Mayoor or people like him?

If you are willing to get something like this still, I really I wish I could do better for you, May Vasudev will bless you.

But if you really believe that there is something wrong in this whole situation. It's time to rethink and get out of this trap.

- We have to understand the true meaning of education and importance of survival in it.

- We have to understand the difference between earning a living, which is something all the creatures in the world are doing and the true meaning of survival, and or earning money which is something only humans are doing.

- We have to understand how these social media people are playing with youth's minds.

- We have to understand how people are doing bad things, to earn pieces of paper called money, like the consultancy people. Like the education sector, which has almost become a business, and Business could be survival, but using people, and calling it survival, it isn't something I could support like every person who puts money ahead of humans, good or bad deeds.

- We have to understand the pureness of the souls of kids, our youth.

They are actually not completely responsible for these cigarettes, alcohol, hook-ups, and abusive culture. Almost everyone is responsible, almost everything is responsible.

A bad mind-set creates a Bad Person.

A bad Person creates a Bad Society.

Bad Societies create Bad Nation.

And do you really think, a Strong Building can be built on a bad foundation?

"Build a strong foundation and you can reach even the most unthinkable heights."

- M. J. Moores

This is one of the reasons, our nation is still developing, and this way, it will always be if we won't do something now.

I really wish I could get some more space to discuss more about solutions to it, but the solution needs discussion with you too. So let's solve this puzzle called life or education, and let's initiate some good discussions around us or here.

Anyways, So, Let's talk about a solution oriented perspective for this, from whole of the discussion the survival should include basic life skills at the minimum, which was somehow there in the initial part of education system. Then somehow which has been removed and any other system got adopted. If we can do something about it is first we can try to make our loved ones teachers to talk about it. Or the best solution here is if there is something we can do as best is, we can try to make out kids learn the basic life skills at the minimum.

Survival is nothing else then surviving the situation. The situation can surely be random, but the necessities should be fulfilled by any situation is called survival. And there are so many things which are required. You must be knowing about it though, Food, water, clothing, sleep, and shelter, these are the basic things for our survival. Somehow our society is teaching that earn money to get these all, but it's not something you can buy always. I would love to add Love, happiness, and peace too into survival. All of these aren't buyable.

Let's solve this through a game, suppose if I would ask you to prioritize these all below words from your perspective, than how would you do that? If want you to write these all words as per your priority, and Put them in the order you would want these.

- Money
- Family
- Career
- Love Life
- Happiness
- Traveling
- Roaming the world
- Job
- Business

- Health
- Peace
- Fitness
- Food
- Home
- Study

"The key is not to prioritize what's on your schedule, but to schedule your priorities."

\- Stephen Covey

You can put anything on your top priority, career, money, and love life, anything you want. Did it?

When you will arrange them in priority, you will notice one thing, that most of the time the things which are below are something you already have, and the things you put above in priority are something you badly need, umm need isn't a good word here, which you want.

Now I want you to ask a few more questions. As

What situations I may have to face to get these in priority?

What skills I may possibly require to get these in priority?

What skill I already have which may need sharpen up?

What assets or things I have got to get these?

What are the things I may need to get these all priorities?

How can I manage them in my life to keep the balance?

The thing is really simple friends, there are two types of houses which most of us usually construct. One is something which is something barely planned, there is almost no floor plan, a mismanaged arrangement of materials, mismanaged people, or man management we may say.

There is one more house, a dream house we may say, before the construction there is proper planning, proper engineer is hired, every detail is being kept in mind and in floor plan as well, there might be 100's of correction until we believe this is going to be the perfect one. Then only we may proceed to the construction. Even after the construction is started we don't just let that happen we plan it to make it better for sure.

"We are never busy, mismanaged though."

- Rahul Bajad

Let me ask you this, which home is going to be better? Off course the planned one? Right? So whatever and however you are going to plan your life is exactly how the life may get there. Depending upon your focus towards it. The main thing is to keep the main thing right.

Lastly and truthfully these all the priorities changes with age and time, ask the same question to any age group the priorities will surely be very different. And if this is something which changes with time. If a thing is something which you would want which is going to loose its priority, than this could be something which is not going to worth one day. Which seems a big worth for now.

There was a line, in hindi from Vikas sir, that

"Yah zindagi jo hai, ye ek jaadu ka khilona he,

Jo mil gya vo maati he, Jo na mila vo sona he."

This means life is a magic toy, Whatever we get we don't respect it in time, and whatever we don't have, we always always and always thinks that is worth. And what we don't have isn't of worth. Did that happen to you as well? From our childhood, our small bicycle, then mobile phone, then a bike, than a car, than a house, than family, than health, than respect? Isn't it something changes with time? I want you to be a person who never ever compromises their soul to something bad deed which your wisdom doesn't approve for any of the things which is going to be changed in our priority later on. I want you to Love and have gratitude for what you have.

I wish you a wonderful and happiest survival. A wonderful education. And a wonderful life ahead.

If there is anything you would like to ask or something please feel free to write directly to me. I will try to respond as much as possible from me.

"Life is all about a Journey, not the goal. Do make sure that the Journey is beautiful than the goal."

- Rahul Bajad

Thank you so very much

Always your well-wisher.

And a small helper to make the world a better place to live.

- Rahul Bajad

Thank you

I would love to first congratulate all, who has completed this book, One thing is for sure that you are really wanting your life and your loved ones life to be better.

I am grateful that you consider reading this book, I would appreciate and request you to use whatever knowledge you gained from my experiences through this book, convert it into a wisdom, and spread as the endless ripple of some powerful discussions of enlightments that could help us to make this world a better place.

Always remember there could be a PLAN B, but I am sure there is NO PLANet B

www.ingramcontent.com/pod-product-compliance
Lightning Source LLC
LaVergne TN
LVHW091147150826
845672LV00005B/1062

* 9 7 9 8 8 9 5 8 8 7 5 3 0 *